The Bible and the Holographic Universe

The Bible and the Holographic Universe

A Christian's Practical Guide to the Universe,
the Multiverse, and the Bibleverse

Cynthia C. Polsley

WIPF & STOCK · Eugene, Oregon

THE BIBLE AND THE HOLOGRAPHIC UNIVERSE
A Christian's Practical Guide to the Universe, the Multiverse, and the Bibleverse

Copyright © 2022 Cynthia C. Polsley. All rights reserved. Except for brief quotations in critical publications or reviews, no part of this book may be reproduced in any manner without prior written permission from the publisher. Write: Permissions, Wipf and Stock Publishers, 199 W. 8th Ave., Suite 3, Eugene, OR 97401.

Wipf & Stock
An Imprint of Wipf and Stock Publishers
199 W. 8th Ave., Suite 3
Eugene, OR 97401

www.wipfandstock.com

PAPERBACK ISBN: 978-1-6667-3558-1
HARDCOVER ISBN: 978-1-6667-9280-5
EBOOK ISBN: 978-1-6667-9281-2

03/30/22

All direct quotations of Scripture are taken from the King James Version (KJV) and are in the public domain in the United States of America.

τοῖς ἐμοῖς φίλοις

To Mom and Dad, who consistently live out the instructions of Deuteronomy 6; to my brothers and G, some of the best friends and contributors anyone could have; and to K, R, E, and C, because, as E would say, "You're the best."

Most of all, "to the only wise God our Savior," to whom "be glory and majesty, dominion and power, both now and ever. Amen" (Jude 25).

"[Reality] is not neat, not obvious, not what you expect."

—C. S. LEWIS

Contents

Acknowledgements | xi
Scripture Abbreviations | xiii
Prologue: Regarding the Universe | xv
Addendum: Four Big Reasons the Holographic Universe Matters | xxi

1 **The Holographic Principle** | 1
    A. What is a Hologram? | 1
    B. The Universe as a Holographic Image | 3
    C. Information: More Than What We Know? | 4

2 **Is the Holographic Principle "Okay" for Christians?** | 8
    A. On Science and Christianity | 8
    B. The Strange Case of Galileo vs. . . . | 10
    C. Christians, and Scientists | 14

3 **Holographic Universes and Meaning** | 19
    A. Life in the Matrix | 19
    B. Choosing the Matrix | 22
    C. The Holodeck | 25
    D. Do Universal Illusions and Reality Matter? | 28

4   **The Bibleverse, a Biblical Perspective of Reality** | 30
    A. A Synopsis of Something Beyond | 30
    B. True Reality | 33
    C. Going Higher | 34
    D. The Real Role of Faith | 37

5   **The Creator Reaches Out** | 39
    A. The Intricacy and Importance of Every Detail | 39
    B. Shadows and Copies | 41
    C. Behind the Veil: Seeing the Throne Room of God | 44
    D. The Message of the Bible | 47

6   **Yearning for Reality** | 50
    A. Perspective and Permanency | 50
    B. Living in Tents of the Body | 53
    C. Investing in the Future | 56
    D. The Origins of Jesus Christ | 59

7   **Time and Knowledge** | 63
    A. The Universe, in 2D and 3D (and 4D) | 63
    B. The Nature of Time (God Knows What You Chose) | 65
    C. A Temporary Universe | 71
    D. Our Limited Understanding | 74

8   **Truth and Substance** | 77
    A. About Absolute Truth | 77
    B. Temporary World, Permanent Reality | 79
    C. Problems of Materialism | 81
    D. From Materialism to Supernatural(ism) | 83

9   **Conforming to Reality** | 86
    A. Information Decay | 86
    B. In the Image, but Not of It | 88
    C. Prayer and Seeking God | 90
    D. Improving the Program? | 92

10 **Origins and Spiritual Illusions** | 96
    A. *The Matrix*, Universal Illusions, and Spirituality | 96
    B. Exploring the Origins of the Holographic Image | 100
    C. Panconsciousness and Panspermia: Self-Generation, Extraterrestrials, and More | 102
    D. The Beginning of the Hologram | 108

Epilogue: Regarding the Multiverse | 111

Appendix A: Where to Learn More about Christianity | 123
Appendix B: How To Be Saved | 124

Bibliography | 129
General Index | 141
Scripture Index | 145

Acknowledgements

THIS BOOK IS THE result of many hours of research, lectures, and conversations. I am thankful to those family members and friends who offered themselves as sounding boards for the incipient ideas that would become *The Bible and the Holographic Universe*, and to others who served as library liaisons during the book's production. Much of what is presented here has grown out of research pertaining to my dissertation on contrafactuals; I would like to thank my professors and colleagues at the University of Kansas and at Yale University for all of their contributions to that work and its ongoing effects. A special thank you to Tom and Nancy for sharing their bookshelves and wisdom. And to my silent beta readers for their patience, comments, and proofreading: you know who you are, and you have my gratitude and esteem.

Scripture Abbreviations

Old Testament

Gen	Genesis
Exod	Exodus
Lev	Leviticus
Num	Numbers
Deut	Deuteronomy
Josh	Joshua
Judg	Judges
Ruth	
1 Sam	1 Samuel
2 Sam	2 Samuel
1 Kgs	1 Kings
2 Kgs	2 Kings
1 Chr	1 Chronicles
2 Chr	2 Chronicles
Ezra	
Neh	Nehemiah
Esth	Esther
Job	

New Testament

Matt	Matthew
Mark	
Luke	
John	
Acts	
Rom	Romans
1 Cor	1 Corinthians
2 Cor	2 Corinthians
Gal	Galatians
Eph	Ephesians
Phil	Philippians
Col	Colossians
1 Thess	1 Thessalonians
2 Thess	2 Thessalonians
1 Tim	1 Timothy
2 Tim	2 Timothy
Titus	
Phlm	Philemon

Scripture Abbreviations

Old Testament

Ps	Psalms
Prov	Proverbs
Eccl	Ecclesiastes
Song	Song of Solomon
Isa	Isaiah
Jer	Jeremiah
Lam	Lamentations
Ezek	Ezekiel
Dan	Daniel
Hos	Hosea
Joel	
Amos	
Obad	Obadiah
Jonah	
Mic	Micah
Nah	Nahum
Hab	Habakkuk
Zeph	Zephaniah
Hag	Haggai
Zech	Zechariah
Mal	Malachi

New Testament

Heb	Hebrews
Jas	James
1 Pet	1 Peter
2 Pet	2 Peter
1 John	
2 John	
3 John	
Jude	
Rev	Revelation

Prologue

Regarding the Universe

Hearing the topic of this book, a very sweet, intelligent elderly friend smiled. "That goes way over my head," she said. She was surprised to hear that she is already familiar with the holographic universe. She deals with it every day, and so do you—though you might not recognize it.

But what is the "holographic universe," and what does it have to do with Christianity? And what does the holographic universe have to do with individual Christians, such as my friend, or you? Does it impact your prayer life, your daily Bible reading, your understanding of faith? That's what much of this book is about, laying the groundwork for viewing the popular science of holograms and alternate worlds with practical application for everyday living. The same insights have meaning for readers wondering how to navigate the popular science and popular culture involving simulated worlds, holographic illusions, and parallel worlds, like those of *The Matrix*, *Star Trek*, Marvel and DC Universes, and so many more. Everything is imparting an ideology. This book is not a primer on popular culture and fiction, but it is a guide to the biblical worldview that allows us to understand and explain our reality, or to what we might call the lens of the "Bibleverse." We need answers; our children need answers; the Bible has answers. Through the Bible, we can tease out the ideologies being ascribed to the holographic universe theory and parallel universes, and separate fact from fiction from science fiction from fantasy.

Prologue

My friend's initial reaction to the phrase "holographic universe" was not unusual. For many Christians, the term is greeted with either curiosity or dismissal. They may have a mild sense of wonder, but think that the subject is entirely abstract. Or they may be overwhelmed at the very notion and immediately wave it away. In the past, as a Classics graduate student studying ancient Greek grammar and narrative, I often met with quizzical responses from people who were not quite sure how the concepts of holographic worlds and alternative universes are relevant, much less what they can mean for Christians. My experiences and research well beyond dissertation completion have only deepened the conviction that we have much to gain from exploring the holographic universe. The entire concept points to a higher reality operating beyond our own and urges us to consider the significance of human life. More importantly, regardless of my personal convictions, it turns out that the Bible addresses the holographic universe. And in very relevant ways.

As for what a holographic universe is, everyone in modern society is completely surrounded by basic examples of the idea. After reading this section, you might set this book down, walk into your living room, and turn on your television. The television is going to show you flat images on a flat screen. These images are two-dimensional. They have height and length, but they do not have any depth. Yet the characters move "around" objects; they move "closer" or "farther away" from items and places. Everything clearly implies a sense of depth.

Let's take it a step further. Assume that you're an actor who portrays a character inside the story you watch on television. When you were watching television, you were watching everything from the outside in, and the world was flat. When you are an actor on the set, you are watching everything from the inside, but you can walk away from the set and leave the story behind. In both of those scenarios, you are not limited by the worlds you are experiencing. You can come and go, leaving the television set and the filming set behind you.

Conversely, if you actually are the character in the world shown on the television screen, and if you truly are the person in the act being performed, the world of the story is your world. Everything around you has depth and meaning. Time passes minute by minute, and you move about within the space of your world, going from one place to another. The world is real to you—never mind that someone who might be watching you on television can never get past the screen to talk with you or shake your hand.

Prologue

The television viewer has a flat experience of your life. You do not. From your perspective, your world is anything but flat.

Although this television analogy does not do the holographic universe full justice, it demonstrates the concept of a higher reality from which our world can appear flat and two-dimensional. We encounter lower "realities" every day when we turn on a television or read a book. Fictional realities are not real in the same way that our world is real, but they can help us to understand a few basics of the holographic universe.

The idea that our universe is a holographic image or a kind of simulated reality is one of the most fascinating modern developments in science. In this view, we are experiencing a world like that of characters inside a two-dimensional television show. The implications of this concept, known as the "holographic principle," are far-reaching and impressive. At first, a holographic universe sounds like an abstract notion. It does not seem to matter much for everyday life. On the contrary, it seems like the plot of a science fiction movie or television program.

At least, that's what the general idea of a holographic universe *feels* like to many people. The truth is that science fiction frequently reflects aspects of the real world, and that this relatively new development in cosmology and physics would be yet another instance in which science fiction has predicted or teased at a hypothetical that could become a known fact. Science fiction's themes of holographic worlds may be kernels of a truth waiting to be discovered.

If it were to move from fictional trope or scientific hypothesis into the realm of recognized fact, the holographic principle would have impact on every area of our lives. Christians are not the only ones who should be aware of the holographic principle. Its consequences affect every human being who has ever lived. If the holographic principle is accurate, then every human being has been living in a gigantic holographic image. The implication is that reality may be nothing like what we think it is. If the holographic principle is accurate, it signals a sweeping change in how we must understand our senses and our surroundings. We think we understand our world based on what we see and experience. This principle undermines the correctness of that understanding from a secular viewpoint as well as from a Christian one. If we are like two-dimensional characters inside a television show and our world is a flat, small-scale reality, what comes next, and who is watching? The Bible has the answers to these questions, but we

Prologue

might not even realize that we need to ask them. They represent a fundamental shift in our point of view.

The nature of this underlying shift is inevitably bound up with our theological perspective. Holographic worlds, alternate realities, and multiverse theory feel far removed from Sunday schools and church services, but as the holographic principle emerges as a theme in our movies and books, and a topic of discussion in our scientific and academic communities, then we have to determine how and where it fits with a biblical worldview. Virtual worlds, unreality, holograms, multiverses appear either fictional and fanciful or separate from our everyday lives. What do concepts like these have to do with real life? How do they fit into what we call "the real world"? What do they even mean, and, perhaps most importantly, what place should they have in our devotions and walk with God? Even if they are not proven, should we shy away from them, or do they contribute to healthy spiritual growth?

As Christians, we should never be afraid to face questions head-on. The huge question of "holographic image or not" is no exception. The sections of this book describe the theory of the holographic principle, discuss how it relates to a biblical worldview in general, and introduce its relevance for personal devotions. It may startle many Christians to learn that the idea of a holographic universe is not so shocking after all—and that it is certainly not a problem for the Bible! The holographic principle fits in remarkably well with the Bible's picture of reality. It is crucial that we understand that the holographic universe idea does not have to be correct in order for the Bible to be true. Still, if the universe is holographic, it is not an issue for the Bible and believers. Actually, the Bible accounts for our seen and experienced reality in a similar way to the holographic principle.

The purpose of this book, then, is to bring the holographic universe theory (holographic principle) out of the domain of abstract science or absurdist science fiction and into the realm of Christian living. To help provide clarity for fellow believers, like my wonderful older friend, who view the holographic universe and so much of the related science and science fiction as things that "go over their heads." To encourage others to delve into the truth of the Bible and to build a deeper, stronger relationship with Jesus Christ. The holographic principle isn't an "answer" to the Bible, because the Bible is the answer to interpreting everything else; the holographic principle isn't a challenge to the Bible, because the real challenge

Prologue

is always aligning our expectations and understanding with what God is telling us in the Word.

The Bible and the Holographic Universe's effects on individual readers are up to the Lord, and are between them and Jesus Christ. The book is designed to be used in multiple contexts: as a series of personal studies, a basic introduction to the holographic universe, a resource raising difficult questions that need to be asked, or a spark for discussion and dialogue in college classrooms, seminaries, and Sunday schools. Small groups and individuals wanting a devotional supplement may find a "forty days" approach useful. It is my hope that however and wherever this book happens to be used, it is a path back to the amazing majesty of the Lord.

In everything, I have worked to pay strict attention to what the Bible says, with the expectation that not everyone will agree with the conclusions or questions discussed here. From the debate between free will/Arminianism and predestination/Calvinism to the nature of time, from the present "weight of glory" to the unutterable glories of the world to come, from the unlimited power of Jesus Christ to the limitations of our humanity, a host of topics are fair game for this discussion—as long as the Bible has the ultimate say. Thanks to God, we don't have to depend on how we feel about points of argument or to live in fear. But don't take it from me. Read the following pages with the Bible in hand. Prayerfully consider everything in light of God's Word, as the Bereans did:

> *These were more noble than those in Thessalonica,*
> *in that they received the word with all readiness of mind,*
> *and searched the scriptures daily, whether those things were so.*
> *(Acts 17:11)*

Addendum

Four Big Reasons the Holographic Universe Matters

Despite its growing popularity, the holographic principle is not something that we as Christians have focused on very much in recent years. With everything going on in the world today, it is especially tempting to think that the holographic principle is nothing compared to biblical prophecy and exegesis. We are living in truly amazing times and watching long-awaited prophecies unfold before our eyes. As foretold by Ezekiel 37–38 and elsewhere, Israel is a nation again, with more Jews flying to the Jewish homeland every year. As predicted in Daniel 9, Revelation 11, and elsewhere, the construction of the Third Temple in Jerusalem is presumably in the near future. In 2020, the life-changing pandemic known as COVID-19 swept across the globe, changing the face of the world in a short time. So who really cares or has time to think about something that feels so far away as a theoretical possibility that the universe is a simulation or a holographic image?

Yet the holographic principle is much more than a passive idea about the fabric of the universe. There are many reasons why the principle is important, not the least of which is that, if true, it tells us more about God's creation around us in the first place. Here are four other reasons for learning about the holographic principle:

1. The holographic principle's insights mesh with biblical information in some very interesting areas, such as the impermanence of the material world (e.g., 1 John 2:17), necessity of laying up treasures in heaven

Addendum

(Matt 6), role of the Tabernacle and priesthood as patterns (Heb 10), and the nature of time (e.g., Ps 39:4–6, 90:4; 2 Pet 3:8). For generations, theologians have argued about predestination versus free will; the holographic principle has some bearing in that debate. The principle has promise for helping us to grasp the spiritual implications of the Tabernacle and Temple as physical models as well. The significance of these complex and fascinating structures can be hard to conceptualize. And the differences between reality here and reality in heaven, sometimes seeming all too remote, only become clearer and better contextualized. Just as the holographic principle is a scientific advancement that only further supports the truth of the Bible, its real existence would elucidate how these sorts of doctrinal points function. Again, the doctrine of the Bible is true, regardless of whether or not the universe is holographic. The clarification achieved by the holographic principle would be like that which we have found regarding ocean currents, the hydrological cycle, and the situation of the earth in space. The Bible makes statements that are accurate. Science displays the physical accuracy of such incidentally scientific statements.

2. The holographic principle is an immediate context for viewing the impermanency of our world. The Bible has always attested that our universe is not the ultimate reality. The world is decaying and has an absolute time at which it will end. Morally, the same decay takes place around us every day. It looks as if society is going insane, caught up in the throes of its own sinful behavior. Why? Because it is. As the Bible says, time is short. The world looks increasingly as if it is falling apart because we are indeed nearing a time when the holographic image will end.

3. The holographic principle is another example of the fact that Christians have nothing to fear from science. We do not have to be afraid. We should be bold enough to explore scientific fact as well as to challenge controversial hypotheses which may or may not be true. The Bible stands up to every test. Showing interest in science does not betray our faith or demonstrate compromise, when undertaken with attention to fact rather than hype or faulty premises.

4. Shying away from the holographic principle only means we will be unprepared to answer questions when they do arise. As the principle gains secular prominence, it will inevitably be raised in theological

Addendum

debates or presented as a supposed challenge to the Bible. First Peter 3:15b directs us to "be ready always to give an answer to every man that asketh you a reason of the hope that is in you with meekness and fear." We cannot be ready to engage with claims if we are not willing to investigate them.

1

The Holographic Principle

Yea, the darkness hideth not from thee;
but the night shineth as the day:
the darkness and the light are both alike to thee. (Ps 139:12)

A. What Is a Hologram?

THE TERM "HOLOGRAPHIC IMAGE" is often popularly conflated with "hologram." Here, I will use the two words "hologram" and "holograph" fairly interchangeably, reflecting their use in popular culture. Technically, the two terms "hologram" and "holograph" denote different elements of holography. A holographic image is like a three-dimensional photograph. When we talk about holograms in casual conversations about science fiction movies or three-dimensional pictures like those on postcards or children's playing cards, we frequently mean holographic images. Merriam-Webster Dictionary describes a hologram as "a picture of a 'whole' object."[1] Science writer Chris Woodford calls a hologram "a cross between what happens when you take a photograph and what happens when you look at something for real."[2]

---

1. Merriam-Webster Online, "Hologram."
2. Woodford, "Holograms."

The Bible and the Holographic Universe

A photograph records patterns of light. The light reflected by a certain object is captured by the photograph, creating a two-dimensional picture of the object. Coined by Sir John Herschel in 1839, the word "photograph" explains the process of taking a photograph. The first half of the word, *photo-*, is derived from the Greek φῶς (*phōs*), "light";[3] the second, *-graph*, is from γράφος (*graphōs*), related to the verb form γράφω (*graphō*): "to write," "to inscribe," or "to draw," all developed from an original sense of "scratch."[4] The process of making a "graph" involves inscribing and drawing or marking. Accordingly, a photograph inscribes and records the light that bounces off an object.

A holograph records light more accurately and realistically than a conventional photograph. While a photograph is flat, a hologram is three-dimensional. It looks as if it has length, width, and height. It can also look as if it is moving in relation to the person who is looking at it. Holograms are created by shining a split laser beam on an object. When we recombine the different parts of the original beam before it was split, we have a recording of how the object appears from multiple angles.[5] The holographic recording captures an image of the object as more than a flat surface in a picture, and as something with depth, shape, and other 3D elements.

A hologram is the imprint produced in the process of recording the holographic image, which, again, is a 3D picture of something.[6] (Notably, as recognized in legal contexts, a holograph is something that is specifically handwritten by its *author*. What does this imply about the *universe* having an author?) The 3D picture of a holographic image is a whole picture. In fact, this terminology reflects the etymology for the word "holograph." The word is taken from the ancient Greek words ὅλος (*holos*), meaning "whole" or "entire," and γράφος (*graphos*), derived from the same verb as the ending of photo-*graph*, γράφω (*graphō*). A holograph is something that is *recorded* in its *entirety*.[7]

---

3. Cf. Liddell et al., *Greek-English Lexicon* (hereafter LSJ), s.v. "φάος."
4. Cf. LSJ, s.v. "γράφω."
5. Holography involves an object wave and a reference wave. The object wave reflects off of the object. The reference wave does not touch the object, but causes interference with the object wave, resulting in a photograph of the whole object. Holographic Studios offers a short explanation of the interference process (Holographic Studios, "Interference").
6. For more information, see Workman, "What Is a Hologram?"
7. Cf. LSJ, s.v. "ὅλος."

The Holographic Principle

B. The Universe as a Holographic Image

The "holographic principle" came to the fore in the 1990s as a response to earlier questions about what happens when information "falls into" a black hole in space. At the time, scientists were working to figure out how black holes fit into the laws of thermodynamics. A black hole is an extremely dense object in outer space. It is created when "so much mass or energy gathers in a small volume that gravitational forces overwhelm all others and everything collapses under its own weight."[8] The material in the object gathers into a tiny condensed area called "the singularity," surrounded by a conceptual threshold between "black hole space" and "normal space." There are at least four different types of black holes.

Originally, black holes presented a problem related to the laws of thermodynamics. According to the first law, conservation of energy, all of the energy in the universe remains constant. Even though energy can change form, it cannot be created or destroyed. The second law describes the process of entropy. Entropy is the increasing disorder in the universe as energy changes into less usable forms. Every time energy is transferred, the transferral involves work. Some energy is lost: it becomes less usable. The universe is always increasing in entropy, moving closer to disorder and reducing its usable energy.

But what about energy and black holes? If everything that goes into a black hole disappears forever, as Einstein's laws of relativity predicted, is the entropy lost? In trying to answer this question through mathematical models, physicists concluded that the second law of thermodynamics is upheld. Their findings also suggested something else that was very interesting: the amount of information inside a bounded physical system, like a black hole, is reflected in the system's surface area. Entropy is related to area, and not to volume. In other words, all of the information contained in the system is encoded on the surface. When it comes to a black hole, what you see really is what you get, because you see on the surface everything that the black hole contains.

This revelation was astonishing. It changes the way we think about information and space. Every bit of information *inside* something that is three-dimensional is actually visible as a two-dimensional picture on the same object's surface. The 3D picture is not what shows from the outside. Instead, it's defined by its 2D boundaries. Someone outside of a contained

---

8. Susskind, "Black Holes," 54.

The Bible and the Holographic Universe

system sees all of the information inside the system like a 2D flat picture, and not a 3D region with shapes and contours. The same principle is thought to apply to the "system" that is our universe and its contents. We may think our world is built of shapes, but from the outside, the shapes are flat, like geometrical planes drawn on a piece of paper.

Of course, our universe has more than two or three dimensions. Time is widely recognized as the fourth dimension. Currently, string theory postulates ten dimensions in the universe.[9] Other more hypothetical versions of superstring theory posit twenty-six dimensions.[10] Chuck Missler has noted that Nachmanides (AD 1194–1270), a scholar of ancient Hebrew, deduced the existence of ten dimensions from studying the book of Genesis alone. Missler gives a possible contextualization for the dimensions:

> There is a provocative conjecture that these ten (or more) dimensions were originally integrated, but suffered a fracture as a result of the events summarized in Genesis chapter 3. The resulting upheaval separated them into the "physical" and "spiritual" worlds . . . The suggestion is that the current physics . . . were a result of the fall.[11]

The study of entropy laws in black hole thermodynamics resulted in significant conclusions about the nature of the universe at large, and as you can see, they pertain to time, space, energy, and the origins of everything. The holographic principle simply takes the lessons from entropy and other physical laws and applies them to the universe as a whole—including humanity.

C. Information: More than What We Know?

Everything in the world we see is made up of stored information.[12] We do not necessarily realize it, but knowing how information is stored and how it appears gives us insight into what the universe looks like and how it operates.

It might seem counterintuitive to think of information in this way. Those of us outside of the computing world tend to speak of information as

---

9. See Sutter, "How the Universe"; and Williams, "Universe." Kaluza-Klein theory argued for at least seven extra or "lost" dimensions; cf. Cramer, "Other 40 Dimensions."

10. Cf. Moffat, *Cracking*, 74.

11. Missler, "Quantum Physics."

12. Compare Alvarez, "What Is the Nature."

The Holographic Principle

facts, such as the distance from Earth to the sun, or the amount of oxygen in the atmosphere. For a visual example of how the universe can be something comprised of information, we may have to turn to something like what is portrayed in the movie *The Matrix*. Even though people inside of the computer-simulated world known as "the Matrix" experience their "world" in real time, the Matrix is really only a stream of computer-generated code. A skilled "operator" who sits in the real world outside of the Matrix can watch green symbols flow across a screen and instantly interpret what is happening inside the Matrix. He understands what the code means. To him, the information-based world of the Matrix makes sense, even though all he ever sees is the code streaming across the viewer. Fascinatingly, operators may never have been inside the Matrix at all. They decipher a code that conveys everything from cars and restaurants to skyscrapers and a blue sky, all of which they themselves have never seen.

In the real world, it is more unusual and challenging to consider our own world as this type of an information-based system. We recall that the material world is made of tiny atoms and quantum bits of some kind, but no one casually observes atoms. We simply don't see bits of information that way.

Still, information is not as restricted to the realms of education or computing as we may believe it to be. Depending on the context, information can refer to various items with effects on or communication about the surrounding world. "Information" may encapsulate a basic knowledge or data acquired through study or some examination, or facts about an event. In genetics, computer programming, and other fields entailing an order of elements (such as a binary code or DNA strand), information is a quality or feature that is inherently demonstrated in, captured by, or conveyed by the elements' particular arrangement.[13] Generally, information can be qualitative or quantitative. It can be used to rationalize a personal decision, form a plan of action, or share an experience.

For our purposes, I'll treat information as individual components of which an object, or more properly, a space, is comprised. To understand how this model of information works, imagine an intricate floor mosaic composed of colored stones. Assume that each stone represents an individual piece of information. Put together, the stones create a picture. The mosaic is the composite "image" of all of the stones it contains. Every stone is an important piece of the picture.

---

13. See Merriam-Webster Online, "Information."

The Bible and the Holographic Universe

In certain contexts, you might look at the stones as subgroups or as individual pieces within the mosaic. You could count the number of stones that are a particular shade of color, for example—the blue ones, or the red ones. Other times you may be more interested in shapes or angles, pointing out the triangular, square, or circular stones, or accounting for how the shapes cooperate to create the whole picture. A single stone might stand out for its unique shade of purple or a strange shape that reminds you of an animal. The stones are individuals, but they also fit into categories based on their attributes.

Nevertheless, when you tell a friend about the experience of seeing a colorful mosaic, you are more likely to describe the full picture rather than the individual stones. The stones are the building blocks of the mosaic. Each one matters, because without them, there is no picture. In practice, though, you speak about the picture as a composite: the result of the pattern or arrangement more than the specifics of the stones used in the process. The composite, the whole, is not the only way you can experience the mosaic's pieces. You can look at them bit by bit and examine the individual stones, or you can analyze stone colors and types. For all that, the one way to see the entire picture is to look at it in its entirety.

The analogy of the vivid mosaic is helpful for grasping the function and importance of information in the holographic universe. Stones equate to pieces of information which create an image when they are all put together. Together, bits of information form the bigger picture—in this case, the picture of the universe. The information is the essence of the image.

Like the mosaic, the holographic image is defined by its information. It is an account of the holographic principle in miniature, relying on informational bits.[14] If everything in a black hole is seen as flat information on the surface, then theoretically, from some vantage point, our universe—also made up of information—appears to be a flat collection of information, too. The surface design of the mosaic may not be obvious to us on the inside. Here, we barely understand the colored stones that are the informational pieces. Where is the vantage point from which we can see the resultant mosaic and appreciate its pattern? From outside the holographic image. That is, from outside our universe.

Meanwhile, inside the universe, the picture is not a flat surface. If it is like a mosaic, the inside does not show the full picture and the colorful arrangement in all of its beauty and intricacy. We may observe some patterns,

---

14. Cf. Minkel, "Sidebar."

but not in their most complete role as they contribute to the mosaic. What we see is more like a storybook: the full story is not visible with the complete meaning of its connected words and sentences. From the inside, the universe has shapes, colors, and contours. It is a 3D world (at least, but of many more dimensions in its full scope)—one that we experience as characters inside it, subject to uncertainty and moment-to-moment suspense—and not a 2D one that we view from the outside, certainly not in its entirety. In the storybook example, the information is the letters, or, going deeper, the smallest dots of ink that are arranged to convey meaning.

Information is the building blocks of the world around us. It is far more than what we see. Our perspective is limited by our position as well as by our sinful human nature. God's perspective, however, is not limited by position or sin. He reveals this uniquely wonderful perspective to us in the Holy Bible. Here we find an unchanging revelation of the true nature of information—all of which is completely visible and comprehensible to the Creator of all things. His Word is a gift beyond our imagination and human interpretation.

2

Is the Holographic Principle "Okay" for Christians?

The works of the Lord are great,
sought out of all them that have pleasure therein. (Ps 111:2)

A. On Science and Christianity

FROM TIME TO TIME, Christians are asked if we fear science. The question routinely is accompanied by the not-so-secret implication that science and facts are supposed to be separate from Christian faith.

Sadly, we who are Christians are often as guilty of dissociating faith and evidence as those outside the church are. A misunderstanding regarding fact and faith pervades the church today. You'll hear the occasional commentator or pastor confidently assert that we need to prioritize faith over science, or that we should ignore whatever threatens our beliefs. Nonetheless, it is a gross misunderstanding to think that science works against faith. Treating faith as if it is baseless or too emotional to be trusted is a disservice to God. His creation and every aspect of its amazing detail reveal the truth of an immutable, faithful Designer. His precepts ring true. His power is unfailing. Our faith works together with fact; we do not have to worry that belief in God's Word will fall short.

Is the Holographic Principle "Okay" for Christians?

> **1** *The heavens declare the glory of God; and the firmament sheweth his handywork.* **2** *Day unto day uttereth speech, and night unto night sheweth knowledge.* **3** *There is no speech nor language, where their voice is not heard.* **4** *Their line is gone out through all the earth, and their words to the end of the world. In them hath he set a tabernacle for the sun.* (Ps 19:1–4)

> *For the invisible things of him from the creation of the world are clearly seen, being understood by the things that are made, even his eternal power and Godhead; so that they are without excuse.* (Rom 1:20)

Naturally (pun intended), scientific hypotheses sometimes make claims that run counter to existing interpretations of the world as we know it. Some hypotheses are proven false, even though scientists or laypeople may be absolutely convinced of their truth. In the eighteenth century, for example, many scientists were convinced that an element known as "phlogiston" was the cause of fire. Phlogiston was supposedly contained by all flammable materials. According to the "phlogiston theory," materials released phlogiston when they burned. This process of releasing phlogiston during combustion was known as "dephlogisticating." Phlogiston remained a serious consideration in chemistry for over a century, until further experimentation and analysis debunked the existence of phlogiston. Nowadays, phlogiston theory belongs to the collection of confuted scientific allegations of the past.[1]

Other hypotheses obviously take the other course and are supportable: entertained by the few or the many, they pass from hypothesis to theory to recognized truth, like the recognition that our solar system is heliocentric or that Earth is round. Whatever the eventual fate of a hypothesis will be, Christians should always be cautious about assuming an antagonistic relationship of science and the Bible in the meantime. Years later, a hostile hypothesis may be proven untrue, so that its apparent contradiction with the Bible never should have posed any issue at all. Problems that arise between the Word of God and the word of science may not be due to "science," but instead to a misunderstanding that is currently called "scientific." The hypothesis might not be true in any sense. On the other hand, the hypothesis might be incomplete, and not yet attaining to true science. In such a case as that, if the hypothesis came to be completely understood, scientists would learn that the earlier interpretation was incorrect. The earlier stages of the

---

1. Phlogiston is discussed in Oxford Reference, "Phlogiston theory"; and Tingle, "Logic of Phlogiston."

The Bible and the Holographic Universe

findings might have appeared to conflict with the Bible because the findings themselves were not complete or understood. The problem, then, was not with the Bible, but with human agents and human (mis)interpretations.[2]

Additionally, during the time before the ultimate outcome of a hypothesis is known (if it can be, depending on the nature of the hypothesis), there are several other points to consider. Does a modern hypothesis really run counter to what the Bible itself says, or merely to current leaders' reading of what they think the Bible says? What political groups are pushing for particular hypotheses to be taught as theory or truth? In the arena of evidence, these questions and others like them matter.

B. The Strange Case of Galileo vs. . . .

One of the favorite illustrations of "Christians vs. Science" is the case of Galileo Galilei and the Catholic Church's opposition to a heliocentric solar system. In the seventeenth century, Galileo's astronomical discoveries and involvement in the debate led to his conviction as a suspected heretic before the Roman Inquisition. Of course, Galileo's support for the hypothesis that Earth revolved around the sun and not *vice versa* was vindicated by later evidence. It is now established fact that Earth does revolve around the sun.

At the time of his trial before the Inquisition in 1633, however, Galileo was in an extremely dire situation. He was accused of defending the Copernican heliocentric theory. This idea that the earth revolved around the sun had been labeled heretical in 1616. Galileo had to side with the church establishment or with his scientific opinion. Forced to recant or face the consequences, he chose to sign the following statement:

> I have been judged vehemently suspect of heresy, that is, of having held and believed that the Sun is the centre of the universe and immovable, and that the Earth is not the center [sic] of same, and that it does move. Wishing however, to remove from the minds of your Eminences and all faithful Christians this vehement suspicion reasonably conceived against me, I abjure with a sincere heart and unfeigned faith, I curse and detest the said errors and heresies, and generally all and every error, heresy, and sect contrary to the Holy Catholic Church.[3]

---

2. See also Mathison, "Bible and Science."

3. As quoted by Shea and Artigas, *Galileo in Rome*, 194. See the full statement and additional analysis in Fahle, *Galileo*, 319–21.

Is the Holographic Principle "Okay" for Christians?

The Catholic Church was not the only religious authority to make the same error. Martin Luther and John Calvin, Reformation fathers, seem to have held to a geocentric view of the solar system.[4] That notwithstanding, human interpretation of Scripture is fallible. The Bible does not clearly address a heliocentric or geocentric system; hence, it is wrong to declare that the Bible condemns the heliocentric theory. The Catholic Church, Luther, Calvin, and established "science" of their time had one view. Galileo had another. Galileo's turned out to have scientific merit. Scripture should not have been used to authorize the heliocentric theory as heresy. Galileo's recantation even pinpoints the source of contention: his view was an "error" and "heresy" that was "contrary to the Holy Catholic Church" (as quoted above). We might say that the statement in this position is entirely, unwittingly accurate: this is a matter of "error" and "heresy" against the Catholic Church institution, rather than against God's Word.

The admission that Galileo was correct did not come until centuries after his death. The nature of this admission again demonstrates that the official contention was between Galileo and Catholic doctrine. In 1822, the Catholic College of Cardinals decided to allow "the printing and publication of works treating of the motion of the earth and the stability of the sun, in accordance with the opinion of modern astronomers . . . in Rome"; and in 1835, at last no longer banned by the Vatican, Galileo's book regarding heliocentrism was removed from the *Index Librorum Prohibitorum* (List of Prohibited Books).[5] Finally, at an official ceremony in 1992, Pope John Paul II acknowledged that Galileo was wrongly convicted. Cardinal Paul Poupard states that the pope was seeking to improve the Catholic Church's public image because it was perceived "as the enemy of science."[6] Notice that the emphasis is on the establishment of the Catholic Church and its position, and not on that of the Bible.[7]

In summary, contrary to common perceptions, Galileo vs. the Catholic Church was never actually a case of Science vs. the Bible. The "Galileo Incident" was about the contemporary institution of the Catholic Church

---

4. Refer to Mathison, "Luther, Calvin, and Copernicus."

5. See Fahle, *Galileo*, notes on 319; Long, "Sept. 11, 1822"; and Vatican Observatory, "Galileo Affair."

6. CNA, "'Galileo and the Vatican'"; Patel, "Vatican Admits"; and D'Emilio, "Pope."

7. Accordingly, in Galileo's 1633 recantation, he echoes the Catholic Church's official and accepted interpretation of the Bible, saying that "it had been *signified* to (him) that the said (heliocentric) doctrine is repugnant to the Holy Scripture" (emphasis mine; quoted in Fahle, *Galileo*, 320).

The Bible and the Holographic Universe

and its interpretation of the Bible. Arguably, every person has some misconceptions about some objective truth somewhere. Any Christian or non-Christian may have a misunderstanding of a physical law or scientific concept. Wrongful perception, confusion, or outright disagreement does not make an objective truth itself untrue. The same statement is true of establishment Catholicism and its view of Earth's situation *vis-à-vis* the Bible.

Without delving too deeply into other questions of doctrine, we can already point to problematic issues with the assumption that Roman Catholicism is biblically Christian *per se*.[8] The existence of this division between established Catholicism and a well-oriented *sola scriptura* worldview (i.e., one that accepts "Scripture alone" as the source of inerrant, revealed truth, guided by the Holy Spirit in absolute consistency with what the Bible says about itself[9]) should reinforce our awareness that modern evangelical church institutions are not responsible for the views of the seventeenth-century Catholic Church—although it is only fair to reiterate that modern Catholics are not teaching geocentric views (and, of course, were not alive in the seventeenth century). Among the issues are the following:

- Lack of recognition that Jesus is the *one and only* way to heaven (as opposed to the biblical emphasis on belief in Jesus Christ as one's Lord and Savior, the only means of salvation; cf. John 1:12, 3:16–17, 3:36, 14:6; Acts 2:38–39, 4:12, 16:31; Rom 1:16, 10:9; Titus 2:11; Eph 2:1–5; 1 John 1:9).

- Works as part of or necessary to attaining the salvation of an individual (as opposed to the biblical teaching that works neither secure nor contribute to salvation, which comes through Jesus Christ alone; cf. Isa 64:6; Eph 2:8–9; Rom 3:20–30, 4:1–7, 9:16, 11:6; Gal 2:16–13, 5:4; 2 Tim 1:9; Titus 3:4–5; Matt 5:20).

- Veneration of humans as formalized saints with the ability to perform mediation between individuals and God, or to intercede on people's behalf (as opposed to the biblical truth that only a single Mediator, Jesus Christ, moderates between humans and God; cf. 1 Tim 2:5; Eph 2:13–22; Rom 3:23, 5:1, 6:23; 1 John 5:11–13).

- Papal infallibility and/or said ability to make declarations with either just as much importance as or more importance than the Bible itself

---

8. See Stewart, "Roman Catholic Claim."

9. For an emphasis on the need for careful individual study and the ability to defend doctrine, consider Patton, "Danger."

(as opposed to the inherent sinful nature of every human being except for Jesus Christ, indicating that no man possesses or receives the right to declare such truth external to the Bible, and opposed to the unchanging authority of God-inspired Scripture; cf. Isa 40:8, 42:8–9; Matt 5:17–18; 2 Tim 3:16–17; Heb 4:12; 2 Pet 1:20–21; Eph 1:21–22; Acts 5:29).

- Worship of Mary, saints, and relics (as opposed to the worship of no one but God alone, in the Godhead of the Holy Trinity of Father, Spirit, and Son; cf. Isa 42:8, 44:6–8, 46:9–11; Exod 20:1–5; Matt 4:10; Rev 19:10, 22:8–9; Acts 10:25–26; Phil 2:9–11; John 5:18, 10:30).
- The doctrine of purgatory and posthumous purification (as opposed to the sufficiency of Christ's Atonement; cf. Isa 53:5; Heb 7:27; 1 Cor 15:3; Heb 9:27; 2 Pet 2:9; 1 Cor 3:10–15; Matt 7:21–23, 12:36; 2 Thess 1:9; Heb 10:12–18; 1 Pet 3:18; 2 Cor 5:6; Rev 20:12–14, 21:8[10]).
- The offering of official indulgences[11] (as opposed to the righteousness which comes through faith in Jesus Christ, indicating that indulgences never are, were, or will be acceptable; cf. Rom 5:9–10, 8:1–11; 2 Cor 5:10–11, 21; Acts 8:20).

Catholicism is therefore not to be so quickly and easily equated with a biblical worldview as many people might believe. Nevertheless, the point is not necessarily about Catholicism and its other tenets of belief, nor is it that Christians (or non-Christians) make mistakes. Again, Protestant leaders Luther and Calvin both evidently shared in the Catholic Church's error regarding geocentrism. The point is that the incident with Galileo was *not* an example of (Galileo and) Science vs. the Bible. In fact, Christianity has a long history of supporting scientific advances. Many brilliant discoveries are the result of research conducted by Christians.[12]

---

10. Refuting purgatory in Hebrews 9:27 and 1 Corinthians 3, see Stewart, "Biblical Support."

11. Compare the ongoing practice of indulgences, as exemplified in a 2017 proclamation (see Chretien, "Church Will Offer").

12. Find more information in Stewart, "Advancement of Science"; and Meyer, "How Christianity."

The Bible and the Holographic Universe

C. Christians, and Scientists

It is no wild claim to say that many scientists have been and are Christians. Quotations from numerous brilliant minds demonstrate the strong influence that Christianity has had on scientific discovery and progression.

Isaac Newton (1643–1727) was one of the greatest and most influential scientists of all time. He is perhaps best remembered for formulating the law of universal gravitation. Newton played a pivotal role in the Scientific Revolution of the seventeenth century (AD). He wrote,

> This most beautiful system of the sun, planets, and comets, could only proceed from the counsel and dominion of an intelligent and powerful Being... This Being governs all things, not as the soul of the world, but as Lord over all; and on account of his dominion He is wont to be called *Lord God* παντοκράτωρ, or *Universal Ruler*.[13]

Newton's contemporary Robert Boyle (1627–91) is known as the first modern chemist, a leading mind in the development of the scientific method. Like Newton, Boyle produced many works of theology. "I think it a duty our reason owes to its Author," he stated, "to endeavour to vindicate his manifold wisdom, in this libertine age; wherein too many men, that have more wit than philosophy or piety, have . . . laboured to depreciate the wisdom of God." Boyle added an expression of a personal desire "that [his] reader should not barely observe the wisdom of God, but be, in some measure, affectively convinced of it."[14]

Michael Faraday (1791–1867) was a pioneer in the field of electromagnetism and, among other things, had an impressive influence on mathematics and chemistry. Citing Romans 1:20a in his scientific lectures, Faraday commented, "I have never seen anything incompatible between those things of man which can be known by the spirit of man which is within him, and those higher things concerning his future, which he cannot

---

13. General Scholium to Newton's *Principia* III (Newton, *Mathematical Principles*, 504; Greek and italics in original). For more on Newton and his beliefs, see the profiles by Lamont, "Sir Isaac Newton"; and Faulkner, "Misplaced Faith." While slightly different in their approaches, these two sources are written under the umbrella of one organization, demonstrating the complexity of Newton's worldview.

14. All quotations from Robert Boyle are taken from his work "A Disquisition about the Final Causes of Natural Things," 515–55, in Boyle, *Works*.

Is the Holographic Principle "Okay" for Christians?

know by that spirit."[15] Faraday similarly remarked that "the book of nature, which we have to read, is written by the finger of God."[16]

Sir William Thomson, otherwise known as Lord Kelvin (1824–1907), is recognized for his work with absolute temperatures (the Kelvin scale) and the laws of thermodynamics. Kelvin said, "If you think strongly enough you will be forced by science to the belief in God, which is the foundation of all Religion. You will find science not antagonistic, but helpful to Religion."[17]

"To me . . . nature in its varied forms are the little windows through which God permits me to commune with Him, and to see much of His glory, majesty, and power by simply lifting the curtain and looking in," wrote inventor, agricultural scientist, and educator George Washington Carver (c. 1864–1943).[18] Asked the secret of his success, Carver commented, "It is simple. It is found in the Bible, 'In all thy ways acknowledge Him and He shall direct thy paths.'"[19]

Wernher von Braun (1912–77), pioneer of rocket technology, declared, "I find it as difficult to understand a scientist who does not acknowledge the presence of a superior rationality behind the existence of the universe as it is to comprehend a theologian who would deny the advances of science."[20]

Such accounts of intellectual pursuits in relation to God and creation are echoed by modern scholars. Just the same, many of today's historians and, yes, scientists attempt to draw sharp divisions between intellectualism and faith. These scholars' portrayal of faith as something that operates in spite of knowledge and curiosity is more than unfortunate. It is an injustice to yesterday's intellectuals and their extraordinary discoveries. Blaise Pascal (1623–62), Carolus Linnaeus (1707–78), Albrecht von Haller (1708–77), William Herschel (1738–1822), Charles Babbage (1791–1871), Matthew Maury (1806–73), James Joule (1818–89), Louis Pasteur (1822–95), James Clerk Maxwell (1831–79), John Ambrose Fleming (1849–1945), Arthur Compton (1892–1962), Ernest Walton (1903–95), and many, many others

---

15. Faraday, *Experimental Researches*, 465 ("Observations on Mental Education").

16. Faraday, *Experimental Researches*, 471.

17. Quoted by Thompson, *Life of William Thomson*, 1099.

18. From "How to Search for Truth," February 24, 1930, to Hubert W. Pelt, as cited in Federer, *George Washington Carver*, 72.

19. As cited in the state of Delaware's 1993 "Statement." See also Dao, "Man of Science."

20. Quoted by Bergman, "Wernher von Braun."

espoused belief in the Bible and/or spoke positively about the relationship between Christianity and scientific pursuits.[21]

Oxford mathematician John Lennox regularly debates atheists and others who attack Christianity in academic and scientific arenas. Recognizing that a Judeo-Christian worldview has been historically associated with scientific development, he points out,

> Recent historians of science . . . are more nuanced in their formulation of the way in which Christian thought influenced the intellectual landscape in which modern science arose, but they reach the same basic conclusion: far from hindering the rise of modern science, *faith in God was one of the motors that drove it.*[22]

"Scientist" and "Christian" are not mutually exclusive identities. The two titles often coincide. Even the famous Albert Einstein made statements to that effect. "I want to know (God's) thoughts," Einstein commented. "The rest are details."[23]

Einstein was not speaking in a vacuum. He was seeking "a theory of everything"—something that could offer a unified understanding of physical laws and nature itself. More recently, speaking from a secular background, Michio Kaku describes the same search: "The physicists of today . . . find ample indirect evidence pointing to the existence of a theory of everything, although at present there is no universal consensus on what this theory is."[24]

Rarely do even Christians realize that we actually have just such a "theory" in the truth of the biblical God. "(The Christian theory of everything) is not the same as claiming we know everything," writes Marc Ambler (Creation Ministries International), "but we do have a framework within which everything in this universe, personal, physical, and spiritual, fits."[25]

---

21. For more examples, consider Morris, *Men of Science*; Graves, *Scientists of Faith*; Lamont, *21 Great Scientists*; and Mulfinger and Orozco, *Christian Men*. See also Camp, "6 Christian Astronauts"; James-Griffiths, "Eighteenth and Nineteenth Centuries"; and Morris, "Bible-Believing Scientists."

22. Lennox, *Can Science Explain Everything?*, 20. Italics in original.

23. Lincoln, "Einstein's Quest." Einstein's comment, based on correspondence reported by Esther Salaman in "A Talk with Einstein," and, noted by Lincoln, inspired Katholieke Universiteit Leuven's exhibition ". . . the rest are details, Einstein 1905—2005."

24. Kaku, *Parallel Worlds*, 187.

25. Ambler, "Biblical Creation."

Is the Holographic Principle "Okay" for Christians?

Theologian and writer C. S. Lewis observes, "Men became scientific because they expected Law in Nature, and they expected Law in Nature because they believed in a Legislator."[26]

The evidence of previous scientists and their discoveries commends us to pursue natural truths from a biblical worldview. Christians can embrace scientific thought, reasoning, and experimentation as a way to learn more about God the Designer and creation the designed. The Lord's character is evidenced in the blueprints and operations of nature. His supreme sense of humor and pleasure, exquisite artistry, and love for detailed, beautiful formulation—all of these personality features of God come across in the testimony of creation. The testimony is readily available to us, because Christianity frees us to explore and investigate without fear.

This is the perspective exhibited by Dr. John D. Morris as he says that "this is a wonderful time to be a Bible-believing Christian/creationist." Morris explains, "The scientific evidence, rightly interpreted, overwhelmingly supports the straight-forward reading of Scripture." He adds that ongoing discoveries only continue to bolster Christian faith in the truth of God's Word.[27]

Science is not supposed to be intimidating for believers, so whether or not the holographic principle is proven, we do not need to fear it. We can potentially learn a lot from considering the implications behind the notion that we live inside a hologram. If we are part of a holographic simulation, *something lies beyond it*. Can the analogy of a holographic universe hint at what it is that lies beyond? Can it lead us back to the higher reality of heaven and spiritual things? Can it lead us back to God? Excitingly, and necessarily, the honest answer is *yes*. The lessons of the holographic universe are not just for physicists and scientists, nor are they restricted to a world of abstractions and mathematical modeling. The lessons of a holographic universe are for the rest of us as well. They have applications for our daily walk with God. This practicality is true not just of the holographic universe theory, but of the rest of creation, too: if we were to begin looking for lessons leading us back to God through awareness of absolute truth in science (and elsewhere), we would find important lessons everywhere.

26. Lewis, *Miracles*, 304.

27. Morris, "Does Science Conflict." See also Answers in Genesis, "Science vs. Religion"; Lisle, "Does Science"; Got Questions Ministries, "Faith in God"; and Slick, "Is Christianity" (listing examples of scriptural consistencies with science, such as ocean currents, Psalm 8; the hydrological cycle, Job [see Neller, "Do You Know?"]; and valleys in the seas, 2 Sam 22:16).

The Bible and the Holographic Universe

Many open-minded physicists and scientists have discovered precisely this same truth. Undoubtedly, many more will continue to discover it as well.

3

Holographic Universes and Meaning

Neither is there any creature that is not manifest in his sight:
but all things are naked and opened
unto the eyes of him with whom we have to do. (Heb 4:13)

A. Life in the Matrix

FOR A MAJORITY OF people outside of the church as well as those inside of it, the phrase "holographic principle" means very little. The science of it tends to mean even less. Indeed, the idea behind the holographic principle is probably more familiar from popular culture than from anywhere else. Mentioning a "holographic universe" regularly evokes images from movies and television.

The holographic universe might be a kind of virtual world or an illusion. Although a holographic universe is not, strictly speaking, a "computer simulation," a computer simulation of some type is in all likelihood the most fashionable or common picture of what a universal illusion might look like. Theoretically, a holographic universe could be a simulated universe, like a huge virtual reality. In the context of computing, "virtual" relates to an immaterial creation that is initiated by and inextricably connected to software.[1] A virtual world is one that does not actually exist, but is programmed and played out on a computer.

One of popular culture's most well-known concepts of a virtual or simulated world is that of the Matrix, from the movie of the same name. In colloquial speech, the Matrix has become essentially synonymous with simulated realities. For that reason, the term "Matrix" many times occurs in conjunction with the holographic principle. In November 2013, the British news site *The Telegraph* ran a story with the eye-catching headline "Do We Live in the Matrix? Scientists Believe They May Have Answered the Question."[2] The article was based on "Do We Live in the Matrix?," a publication by *Discover Magazine*. Author Zeeya Merali uses the Matrix as a starting point to explain the theory that human beings may live inside a gigantic virtual universe. In a short discussion of the "simulation hypothesis," Merali notes that the idea is no stranger to philosophy. Numerous philosophers over the years have maintained that human beings represent forms of artificial intelligence. In these proponents' views, humans are caught in a simulated world, and are virtual rather than organic.[3]

The Matrix, the first movie of the famous franchise, was released in 1999. The film regularly appears on lists of best science fiction movies.[4] Two sequels, *The Matrix Reloaded* and *The Matrix Revolutions*, followed in 2003. Considered largely unimpressive by fans, the last two movies in the trilogy still left a large cultural impact.[5] The story has not ended there: in August 2019, over fifteen years since the release of the original movie in the franchise, *The Matrix 4* was announced. Originally dubbed "Project Ice Cream," *The Matrix Resurrections* suffered quickly under the changing reality of a world struck by COVID-19. Its release date was shifted from May 2021 to April 2022 before making its way back to December 2021.[6] The movie's reception prior to release constantly demonstrated that American culture is increasingly accepting of the idea that reality is not all that simple after all. In 2021, moviemakers and certain reviewers predicted that viewers would

1. Lexico, "Virtual."
2. Kinder, "Do We Live."
3. Merali, "Do We Live."
4. Libbey, "30 Best Sci-Fi"; Huddleston and de Semlyen, "100 Best Sci-Fi"; Fischer, "50 Greatest Sci-Fi"; and Heritage, "Matrix."
5. Wojnar, "5 Best (& 5 Worst)"; Whitney, "15 Years Later"; Lawlor, "10 Reasons"; and Harrison, "What Went Wrong."
6. Elvy, "Predicting"; and Marshall and Perry, "Matrix Resurrections"; and IMDb, "Matrix Resurrections."

find the Matrix as relevant as ever. "The deeper themes at work, about the growing sense that our world is fundamentally an unreal one, could click perfectly with viewers upon the film's release," said David Sims (*The Atlantic*), shortly after the sequel's announcement.[7]

The premise of the original *Matrix* trilogy is that the universe is actually a massive computer simulation. Nearly every human being in *The Matrix* is plugged into the "Matrix" simulation from infancy. Unwittingly, these people live their entire lives in a program created by Machines invisible to them. Hardly any humans know the truth about the simulation and the Machines. Those who do are forced to fight for their existence in the dingy and dangerous real world, where they face the daily perils of murderous mechanical "Sentinels."

On the inside, the Matrix is the everyday world we know, complete with cities and parks, work schedules and schools, traffic and entertainment, family and friends. Insiders typically pass their entire lifetimes without knowing that their world is artificial. They do not see the code for what it is, nor do they ever see their world for what it truly is.

From the outside, the Matrix looks like nothing more than a series of minute green characters falling across a flat black computer screen. Characters rescued from the Matrix can re-enter the simulation by literally plugging back into its stream of code. As characters plug into the Matrix, they instantaneously appear back in the three-dimensional world of the computer program. Their appearance and abilities inside the Matrix can be completely different from those outside of it—in the other, "real" world. Their bodies remain outside the simulation, but their virtual self-representations simultaneously exist inside the Matrix. They make conscious decisions and control their bodies in the Matrix as if it is the real world.

Do we live in the Matrix? According to the Bible, the answer is no. Even if we live in a holographic simulation, the Bible demonstrates how our idea of reality fits together with a higher reality we cannot see or understand. We do not live in the massive deception of a simulated world like that of the Matrix. Truth *can* be known, and the Creator is not attempting to hide it or reality from us. God makes the truth known: what we experience here on Earth, although it may be like a gigantic illusion or a running simulation, has real impact on eternity. Jesus died on the cross for real. His death mattered. He rose from the dead for real. His resurrection brought

---

7. Sims, "*Matrix 4*."

The Bible and the Holographic Universe

the opportunity for eternal life to all who would choose to accept Jesus as Christ and Lord, the perfect and necessary Atonement for sin.

By contrast, in the *Matrix* franchise, most events that happen in the Matrix never really take place. Humans are never physically in the world constructed by the computer. They dream it and live out fake lives in the fake world, all the while being tended by Machine farmers in the real world. The majority of people pass their physical lives in an unseen reality dominated by sinister Machines. This construct is very dissimilar from the reality revealed to us in the Bible. The Bible shows that our world is impermanent, yes. Yet this world is not a figment of an artificial intelligence's imagination, and it is not like a dream. We will not wake up sometime and discover that it all "never happened." What we will discover is that the realm we know is a very small and very transient reality. We are surrounded by an immense, permanent spiritual world. While our physical experiences prior to eternity are real, our limited view and understanding constrain us, so that we do not have the ability to fully understand how our physical world operates within reality. God's Word reveals critical information to us regarding our place, the nature of our world, and the higher reality that lies outside of what we are able to see and comprehend.[8]

B. Choosing the Matrix

The Matrix is one version of a simulated universe. Its inhabitants are by and large involuntary inmates of a gigantic unseen prison. The few exceptions are people who "opt in" to the life offered them in the Matrix. They prefer to deny the reality of what the Matrix is. While they do not feature prominently in the movies, we see at least one of them in the first film of the franchise. This character, a villain, explains his reasoning in a scene where he sits eating a (simulated) meal inside the Matrix. He realizes that the food before him is completely imaginary. Why choose the Matrix, then, if it is meaningless and nothing? Because, he has decided, it is better to know nothing about reality and to enjoy the unreality. His logic can be easily summed up in the statement that *what he does not know* (he believes) *will not hurt him*.[9]

---

8. See also Lisle, "How Do I Know."
9. The Character Quotes, "Cypher."

Holographic Universes and Meaning

Elsewhere, the same character affirms the choice to live in the Matrix. His view is simple enough. He prizes the fake reality as a *higher* reality.[10] This fictional character is making a choice to embrace fiction. He would rather live in the fake world because the real world is so comparatively bleak. It is a harsher place to live than the Matrix is. Certainly, viewers can readily agree on that point. The real world of *The Matrix* would be a very hard place to live. The character's worldview is considered so pervasive and even persuasive that an entire fictional group bearing his name arises after him in the multiplayer role-playing game *The Matrix Online*, making related arguments that humans would be better off never awakening to the truth of the Matrix and Machines.[11] Interestingly, the actor who portrays the character has defended the decision as well, arguing that the logic makes sense for someone in that position.[12]

Beyond the franchise, video gamers in particular have noted their willingness to enter a Matrix. Some of them give similar reasons to those named by the character as he eats his fake meal. Mark Silcox, department chair of humanities and philosophy at the University of Central Oklahoma and a former gamer, speaks of his own willingness to leave the real world behind: "I mean, my view of the Matrix is: If it were really that easy to go into it—and it wasn't of course run by an evil empire robot—I'd be all for it. I'd plug it in in a second."[13] Silcox even refers to philosopher Nick Bostrom's theory that our lives are a virtual reality simulation (discussed below). "If there's a 33 percent chance that what I call reality is virtual, then what's the stuff that I call virtual?"[14] And like the *Matrix* villain who finds the Matrix "more real" than what lies outside of it, gamers in certain contexts contend that virtual reality is just as or more meaningful than the world beyond. "What is a real world?" asks one self-described gaming addict.[15] Video gamers like these echo the sentiments of the *Matrix* character in

---

10. The Character Quotes, "Cypher."
11. Matrix Wiki, "Cypherites."
12. Fuge, "Why Cypher." Various philosophers debate the morality of the character's decision, however, some concluding that it is inherently immoral (cf. Erion and Smith, "Skepticism").
13. Tourjée, "Real Life."
14. Tourjée, "Real Life."
15. Tourjée, "Real Life." Another account of an addicted gamer describes a young man who found life "saturated with meaning" in the world of his game. "I envy this experience as much as I fear it," remarks the man's friend (Guan, "Why Ever Stop").

The Bible and the Holographic Universe

their willingness to enter the Matrix. The choice may be less physical and more abstract, but no less present.

In a larger example of the choice to "plug in" to the Matrix, a group of approximately 650,000 users on Reddit have built an entire subcommunity ("subreddit") where life is treated as a gigantic video game called "Outside." The subreddit's "About" section pronounces reality "a free-to-play MMORPG [Massively Multiplayer Online Role-Playing Game] with 7 billion+ active players."[16] Here, our world becomes a massive game. COVID-19 is a "bug" in the 2020 version, ages are levels, and events are "minigames." One anonymous user sheds light on how he uses the game concept to escape from probing questions of theology and God's existence. By "gamify(ing)" such frightening uncertainty about God and the nature of his own place in the universe, the gamer creates a distance between himself and harsh questions about his own reality. As a result, these questions do not carry the same weight for the person who is playing the game. They become important questions for the gamer's character. In other words, by transferring questions about God over to the game, the gamer can avoid worrying about God nearly as much. The intimidating issues of life and afterlife become his character's concern.[17]

Resorting to a "Matrix" or "virtual game" framework feels safe(r) and may carry a sense of belonging. Professor Katia Samoilova, who studies philosophy and video games professionally, observes that the name "Outside" conveys a sense of security that gamers can find inside of the safe confines of the gameworld. Connecting with the game is also a means for connecting with other people in a safer space, meaning that the game functions as a comparatively controlled way to relate with the real world and real people.[18] This level of gamification translates the decision of choosing the Matrix from the level of abstract thought experiments to that of concrete life experiences, where adults deliberately reject our world and act on that rejection.[19]

16. Reddit, "Outside," section "About Community."

17. Andrews, "What If."

18. Andrews, "What If." Samoilova teaches on philosophy through video games at California State University, Chico. Students' responses are explored by Souders, "New Class."

19. This strong reaction of gamers represents a form of skeptical role-play, where those who deny, doubt, or refuse the reality of our world are actually able to act on emotions like those of the *Matrix* villain (as opposed to an abstract and untenable skepticism; cf. Erion and Smith, "Skepticism," 27).

Holographic Universes and Meaning

The ability to dictate the level of reality that they are willing to experience offers people an impression of increased control over their own outcomes. These gamers do not have to dwell on the reality of God or wade through questions about the meaning of life. Instead, through a choice to engage with life as they would with a virtual reality, real human beings can try to assert—like the character in *The Matrix*—that it is better not to know of reality than to be trapped in a reality that is dangerous, despicable, or otherwise undesirable.

C. The Holodeck

Video gaming and the decision to live in something akin to the Matrix evoke another familiar portrayal of a simulated universe: *Star Trek*'s "holodecks." In these creative fabrications of worlds, participants enter into a simulation of their own choosing. Holodeck users are comparatively like modern gamers. They enter and leave the holodeck at will. They frequently possess more power than today's gamers, because holodecks are more easily manipulated by individual users. Except in certain situations, the parameters of holodeck "programs" can be altered by voice command or slight manual adjustments. Like the Matrix, however, holodecks can trap their users inside of simulations. Simulations can go awry or be maliciously reprogrammed, and when they do or are, they can cause injuries and death. Yet the holodeck, dissimilar to the Matrix, is intended for relatively innocent purposes. Holodecks are mainly used for good throughout the *Star Trek* franchise.

In appearance, holodecks are large rooms with yellow grids on black walls. An activated "hologrid" projects immersive scenes that surround the users.[20] While the Matrix is more like a prison than a realm of escapist fantasy, the holodeck captures a futuristic essence of today's world of virtual reality and video games. It is associated with entertainment or information. Holodecks are places where *Star Trek* characters step into the worlds of their favorite books or films, experiment with technological innovations, play through "what if" scenarios to make decisions about real life, and create imaginative worlds of other kinds. And occasionally, regrettably, characters do become trapped by haywire computers, evil alien entities, or other humans (among other things).

---

20. Further described in Memory Alpha, "Holodeck."

The Bible and the Holographic Universe

Holodecks are primarily sources of entertainment and inspiration, and sometimes of terror and disorientation. The nature of their use truly depends on the simulation, user, and general situation. One interesting feature of the holodeck is its priority of user safety, something very foreign to the Matrix. In *Star Trek*, holodeck users have the option of turning on "safety protocols." When safety protocols are activated, users can expect to interact with the simulated world without worry. They are not threatened by the worlds they experience and shape.

In the computer-simulated universes of both the Matrix and the holodeck, simulations can be deceptively real. In *The Matrix*, "users" are almost always caught inside the simulation. They are prisoners, not game players. They neither possess knowledge of the Matrix nor assent to its laws. They are never asked their permission; they are simply subject to the Matrix from birth. The Matrix is a full world with boundaries and limitations. Only those who are on the outside see the Matrix for what it is.

Even so, users who do agree to enter into the Matrix almost universally experience it as a real world. Their bodies are outside of the Matrix, but their minds are inside it. They suffer when they are injured, enjoy the tastes of various foods, and die in the real world when they are killed inside the simulated one. The connection between the Matrix and reality is invisible. The former is extremely duplicitous and just as deadly to its inhabitants; the latter is dark and dangerous. People who live outside of the Matrix are always on the edge of extinction.

Conversely, in *Star Trek*, users habitually recognize the truth when they are inside the world of a holodeck.[21] They have knowledge of the holodeck's existence. They commonly look forward to entering the holodeck. To them, it is a place to escape from the real world, and it is more often a site of fun diversion than of danger or fear. Characters feel safe inside a holodeck because they believe that they can always leave or control their imaginary circumstances. For instance, on one occasion when a starship captain is running a simulation about a 1940s mystery and playing the role of a stereotypical private detective, a holographic police lieutenant warns him against trying to abscond. The captain and the audience can both be amused at the admonition. If the captain were to flee by exiting the holodeck, there would be no city or police department at all.[22]

---

21. See also Kennedy and Kennedy, "Holodeck."

22. As featured in *Star Trek: The Next Generation*, "The Big Goodbye"; with additional details in Memory Alpha, "Big Goodbye," section "Memorable Quotes."

Holographic Universes and Meaning

The nature of the holodeck's unreality can be forgotten in the most persuasive simulations, merely because the simulations are so realistic. Still, most of the time, characters remember that they are in a holodeck. They find comfort and pleasure in realizing the boundaries of the simulations. Since they control the qualities of the virtual worlds, they have a sense of power. The majority of those in the Matrix have nothing comparable.

Sometimes, the virtual reality of the holodeck elicits bigger questions about reality. Later in the same episode with the 1940s mystery, Captain Picard has convinced a holographic policeman that the world of the holodeck is not as real as it appears to be. Before Picard leaves, the lieutenant asks him a poignant question. What will remain after Picard exits the holodeck and ends the program? The holographic character anxiously wants to know what will happen to his family and the rest of the world he thought he knew. Unfortunately, Captain Picard can offer no real assurance. He realizes that he has no answer to give, because he actually has no framework for thinking of the computer simulation in this deeper sense. The previous joke of evading a non-existent police department has serious undertones. All Picard can do is admit that he has no idea of what, if anything, he will leave behind.[23]

Again, unlike the Matrix, the cases when characters do not give assent to being inside the holodeck are comparatively rare. We may see occasional episodes in which characters are trapped in a simulation, but these scenarios are relatively few in comparison with the vast numbers of times when the holodeck is used for entertainment or training. The holodeck is clearly not a real world at all, even though it can affect characters on a very meaningful level. Still, unless the "safety protocols" are turned off, the holodeck's impact is limited. A holodeck experience leaves more of an emotional mark than a physical one. It influences reality for the characters by transforming their perspectives, giving them experiences and new memories, and changing their lives. But in the end, the holodeck is a holodeck, and it isn't *real* reality—or at least, it isn't the highest reality. If it is real, it is *less* real than the main material world of *Star Trek*. Stepping off of a shuttle onto a new planet means encountering aliens and taking risks. Stepping into a holodeck and into a new world means encountering a computer-simulated world governed by regulations, programs, and technological limitations.

---

23. See IMDb, "Patrick Stewart," section "Quotes."

The Bible and the Holographic Universe

D. Do Universal Illusions and Reality Matter?

The two examples of the simulated worlds in *The Matrix* and *Star Trek* are not exactly what we might call "holographic universes," but they are two examples of types of universal illusions. They also raise intriguing points about interactions with unreal worlds. In both of them, time passes while characters are passing time inside the simulations. In both of them, users may feel as if they are crossing vast spaces or performing physical activities—traveling on vehicles, running, climbing, or eating, for instance—even though the characters themselves have either not moved at all in the real world (as in *The Matrix*) or are moving within a limited space (as in holodecks). If we turn from these fictional universes (and, for that matter, from virtual reality in gaming) to real life, where can we find analogues for a holographic universe? And how is the idea of a "holographic universe" relevant for us, knowing that we are neither trapped by the Matrix's energy-craving Machines or sheltered within the walls of a "safety"-engaged room on a spaceship?

Relevance is exactly the question posed by a 2015 article provocatively titled "Some Physicists Believe We're Living in a Giant Hologram—and It's Not That Far-Fetched."[24] Author Joseph Stromberg asks how it would affect the habits of our daily lives if it were to be proven that the universe were only a holographic image.

The answer is complex. Given that physical laws would not change, knowing that we live in a holographic world would not have an apparent effect on our daily lives. Gravity would continue; the sun would still appear to rise in the morning and set in the evening. The laws of thermodynamics would proceed as regularly as always. Materially, the universe would seem unchanged. How, then, would the discovery matter? Stromberg emphasizes that the major difference would be an intangible one. If we were to learn that our universe truly is holographic, then we would be closer to understanding the nature of the physical laws that govern our everyday life.[25]

On a physical level, the laws of physics control our actions in that they determine what we can do and how. They regulate and describe gravity, inertia, momentum, electromagnetic energy, growth and decay, light and darkness, and even other essentials of life, such as breathing. These physical realities direct our environment and our relationship with it. In many ways,

---

24. Stromberg, "Some Physicists."
25. Stromberg, "Some Physicists."

they also direct our interactions with each other. As such, these laws do not have any bigger claim on any one person than on another. They simply exist. We operate within their boundaries, like the parameters set for people in the Matrix or the confines set by the holodeck's current programming.

Granted, even if everyone on Earth believed we were living in a holographic universe, nothing would appear to change. Shapes would appear as three-dimensional as ever, time would feel as four-dimensional as it always has to us, and flat things would still look flatly two-dimensional. But the holographic principle does have an impact on our worldview as well as on our ultimate physical existence. Obviously the gamers building a community of "Outside" players, where real life is nothing but virtual reality, treat virtuality as another kind of space. The world as a game is a place for them to think differently. It may serve as a "safe space" to avoid profound thoughts at all. A sense of reality as "unreal" would inevitably alter our view of life. For that reason alone, if for no other, the holographic principle should only continue to draw attention and significance.

Nonetheless, as quickly as we might find solace in believing our world is virtual and *unreal*, we should questions what that conclusion would mean. "Unreal" is not the same as "*less* real" or "ineffective." We know that the world we live in changes us and has real effects. The Bible explains that the decisions made in this world determine our eternity. We cannot shut down the simulation of our lives and walk away, or verbally command a computer to recalibrate. Just because our reality is ruled by a higher reality does not cause everything to become meaningless; instead, in a way, everything becomes more meaningful, because the smallest details of life have a difference for who and what we will become when the universe comes to its final end. The Bible speaks of "redeeming the time" (Eph 5:16a) because we can make future investments that will live beyond this short-lived universe. Realizing that our daily tasks are so fundamentally important can inspire hope if we see everything as a deliberate aspect of a reality designed for bigger things.

4

The Bibleverse, a Biblical Perspective of Reality

He revealeth the deep and secret things:
he knoweth what is in the darkness,
and the light dwelleth with him. (Dan 2:22)

A. A Synopsis of Something Beyond

Writing around AD 61–62, the apostle Paul makes a profound statement that encapsulates his entire approach to Jesus Christ and the meaning of life itself: "To me to live is Christ, and to die is gain" (Phil 1:21).[1] Paul's declaration is as expressive as it is concise. He knows what it means to live an abundant life and to face a violent death. He is addressing the Philippian believers from his house imprisonment in Rome.

Paul describes his choice to continue living in the world as a struggle.

> **22** *But if I live in the flesh, this is the fruit of my labour: yet what I shall choose I wot not.* **23** *For I am in a strait betwixt two, having a desire to depart, and to be with Christ; which is far better:*

---

1. "This is the philosophy of Christian living: To live Christ; to die gain" (McGee, *Philippians–Colossians*, 35). An overview of the book of Philippians is available on Grace to You, "Philippians."

The Bibleverse, a Biblical Perspective of Reality

> **24** *Nevertheless to abide in the flesh is more needful for you.* **25** *And having this confidence, I know that I shall abide and continue with you all for your furtherance and joy of faith;* **26** *That your rejoicing may be more abundant in Jesus Christ for me by my coming to you again. (Phil 1:22-26)*

Paul is not being suicidal or morose. He is being realistic. He realizes that our world is transient. The reality we see isn't going to last. We all recognize the world's impermanence in facing the existence of death. From childhood, people are aware that human beings, like all other things in our world, decay and eventually die. Death cannot be escaped or outrun.

But death is not the "end of the road." The Bible explains that there is something that comes after life on this earth. Each human soul has a destination that is permanent, even if the world itself is temporary.

What we do on Earth matters because of our relationship with eternity. We are creatures with souls that will exist forever.

> **13** *Every man's work shall be made manifest: for the day shall declare it, because it shall be revealed by fire; and the fire shall try every man's work of what sort it is.* **14** *If any man's work abide which he hath built thereupon, he shall receive a reward.* **15** *If any man's work shall be burned, he shall suffer loss: but he himself shall be saved; yet so as by fire. (1 Cor 3:13-15)*

What work endures? Only that which is done for the glory of God. "And the world passeth away, and the lust thereof: but he that doeth the will of God abideth for ever," as John assures us (1 John 2:17). Even though we may want to appease the world and feel good about what happens here, works done for the sake of pleasure or worldliness do nothing to guarantee a positive eternal result. According to the Bible, only our relationship with Jesus Christ decides what our individual futures look like.

Later in the letter to the Philippians, Paul emphasizes that everything that might appear to give confidence in the flesh—everything tied to this passing reality—counts as nothing at all in itself.

> **7** *But what things were gain to me, those I counted loss for Christ.* **8** *Yea doubtless, and I count all things but loss for the excellency of the knowledge of Christ Jesus my Lord: for whom I have suffered the loss of all things, and do count them but dung, that I may win Christ. (Phil 3:7-8)*

Verses like these reflect the true nature of our relationship to the physical world around us. The message of physical imperfection and impermanence is all over the Bible. "For we are strangers before thee, and sojourners, as were all our fathers: our days on the earth are as a shadow, and there is none abiding" (1 Chr 29:15).

It turns out that the reality we think we are living in is not the primary world. We shouldn't aim our efforts at pleasing the world or planning to live in it forever. Does this mean we should seek to die, so that we can reach a permanent world more quickly? No; our times are always in God's hands, and not in our own (Ps 31:15a). Paul is saying that we should choose to live. How? For one thing, by going back to God's promise in Deuteronomy 30:

> **19** *I call heaven and earth to record this day against you, that I have set before you life and death, blessing and cursing: therefore choose life, that both thou and thy seed may live:* **20** *That thou mayest love the Lord thy God, and that thou mayest obey his voice, and that thou mayest cleave unto him: for he is thy life, and the length of thy days: that thou mayest dwell in the land which the Lord sware unto thy fathers, to Abraham, to Isaac, and to Jacob, to give them. (Deut 30:19–20)*

Both the physical Promised Land of Israel and the promise of rest associated with it are a representation of eternal inheritance in Christ. God works with patterns and illustrations. His dealings with Israel are, among other things, a pattern and illustration. The promise of a homeland, rest, and other good things from God are a pattern for the abundant life Christians can continue to have when we seek God first. Like the Tabernacle and priesthood, which teach immutable truths about God and the relation between God and humanity, the promise of Deuteronomy 30 is a pattern. God blesses and fulfills those who choose life in Christ. And the promise is bigger than anything here in the moment and in the material world.

The secular world, starting to publicly acknowledge its impermanence, is beginning to catch up with the Bible's teaching of an illusory world. It isn't that scientists have missed the idea that our physical world is running down; the laws of thermodynamics have long described the effects of decay and increasing disorder in the universe. The holographic principle is another discussion that inevitably leads to questions about the universe as a place that does not last forever.

Our world's relative "unreality" would hint that the universe could disappear about any time. The Bible has gotten it right again: the world is transient, and while it is our reality now, it will not always be. If it weren't for biblical prophecies still to be fulfilled before the end of the world, we might even look for the holographic image to terminate at any time. The image is degrading, not developing toward a "better" shape of itself.

B. True Reality

The entire Bible emphasizes that we have a promise of life and meaning well beyond ourselves. Accordingly, the degradation and unworthiness of our current universe come through in the disciples' interactions with Jesus throughout the Gospels. We need salvation because we are insufficient in ourselves, and because this reality is just as insufficient as we are. Along those lines, it is a true glimpse of reality that Jesus' disciple Philip requests in John 14:

> **8** *Philip saith unto him, Lord, show us the Father, and it sufficeth us.* **9** *Jesus saith unto him, Have I been so long time with you, and yet hast thou not known me, Philip? he that hath seen me hath seen the Father; and how sayest thou then, Show us the Father?* **10** *Believest thou not that I am in the Father, and the Father in me? the words that I speak unto you I speak not of myself: but the Father that dwelleth in me, he doeth the works.* **11** *Believe me that I am in the Father, and the Father in me: or else believe me for the very works' sake.* (John 14:8-11)

Jesus' reply to Philip builds on another famous verse from the chapter, when Jesus is revealed to be "the way, the truth, and the life" (John 14:6). He shows us what it means to find the path to true reality. He, Jesus Christ, is it.

At this point, some readers might ask a big question. Since every soul outlives the holographic universe, doesn't everyone ultimately go to a higher reality outside of this simulation? The answer is yes and no. Yes, every human soul will survive beyond the simulation. No, not everyone will go to the true, higher reality that is desirable.

The supernatural reality is that each individual human is presented with a choice between eternity in heaven or in hell. These two destinations are the only two choices, and the Bible is clear about the stark contrast between them. Heaven is a place of eternal life. The soul who goes to heaven outlives the holographic universe for good. Hell, on the other hand, is a place of eternal death. Souls who go to hell are forever condemned. Having rejected God, they are separated from all goodness.

The Bible and the Holographic Universe

Reality being what it is, the old maxim "All roads lead to God" is true. However, not all roads lead to *heaven*. All roads lead to the Throne of God. For believers, seeing God on the Throne will be a commendation: a time of joy, when we receive rewards for good deeds. For unbelievers, encountering God on the Throne is a condemnation: a time of grief, where the nature of justice demands punishment for sins. Every person will one day be rewarded for deeds committed within the hologram (e.g., Jer 17:10; Matt 16:27; 2 Cor 5:10; and Rev 22:12). God "will render to every man according to his deeds" (Rom 2:6).

Only one road has a positive destination for the few travelers who take it. In the words of Christ,

> **13** *Enter ye in at the strait gate: for wide is the gate, and broad is the way, that leadeth to destruction, and many there be which go in thereat:* **14** *Because strait is the gate, and narrow is the way, which leadeth unto life, and few there be that find it.* (Matt 7:13-14)

The theory of a holographic universe not only emphasizes that we cannot expect this world to go on forever, or even that everything material does not endure; it also underscores the need for a real, lasting salvation. Jesus Christ fills the need for salvation for everyone who will believe. The belief is not in just anything or anyone. It must be in Jesus Christ, as the Savior. That is the cohesive, comprehensive worldview of the Bibleverse, the reality of which we are assured by the Bible.

C. Going Higher

After we are saved, striving after reality is a mindset that calls for discipline. We see the real world more clearly through a daily practice of straining after the things of God. In Philippians 3, the apostle Paul spells out what such straining should look like in everyday life. He tells us to focus on our future in Jesus Christ instead of dwelling on the past. Remarkably, Paul speaks of "forgetting those things which are behind, and reaching forth unto those things which are before" (Phil 3:13b).

The word for "reaching forth" in verse 13 is ἐπεκτεινόμενος (*epekteinomenos*), from ἐπεκτείνω (*epekteinō*), "to extend beyond," derived from the literal action of "stretching out." This verb means "to reach forward" and "to stretch out," as if exerting ourselves to grasp after something. Paul means to inspire us to think about our actions less passively and more purposefully. Instead of waiting for the future to come, like bystanders who watch as events unfold, we are encouraged to be deliberate about our relationship with Christ. Mainly, ἐπεκτεινόμενος is an expression of how we should push ourselves toward a better, stronger Christian walk by being intentional about our everyday choices. "Reaching forth" in the sense described by Paul is reaching out as *far* as we can to know Jesus as *much* as we can. It is a process of surrendering. Rather than putting our efforts into following and fulfilling our own desires, we should be pouring ourselves into following Jesus. His pleasure ought to be our goal. As we strive to do what pleases our Savior, we'll find that our desires come to align with the holiness of God. His desires become our own—because we are gaining a proper focus of what "good," "desirable," "holy," and "worthy" really mean.

What does ἐπεκτεινόμενος/*epekteinomenos* have to do with the holographic universe? In verses 14–15, Paul communicates an essential truth: mature Christianity recognizes that there is an external reality, and that it is what holds actual importance. And so a mature Christian like Paul works to forget the past. Forgetting the past does not mean forgetting the lessons learned from past mistakes or successes, but not being caught up with those mistakes, and not boasting in those successes. Most importantly, mature Christians recognize that status and acclaim in this world mean nothing in the next.

Forgetting the past is a process of focusing on the future. Paul describes his personal experience of reaching forward to the future, and thus embracing the external reality of the spiritual world:

> **14** *I press toward the mark for the prize of the high calling of God in Christ Jesus.* **15** *Let us therefore, as many as be perfect, be thus minded: and if in any thing ye be otherwise minded, God shall reveal even this unto you.* (Phil 3:14–15)

In Greek, the word rendered as "perfect" in verse 15 is τέλειοι (*teleioi*). It means "accomplished" or "complete"; in reference to animals and to humans, it can also mean "full-grown."[2] Essentially, what is "complete" is developed and mature. Mature, developed Christians are those who overlook the things of the world and turn their eyes to the eternal calling of life in Jesus.

Verses 4–6 note that striving ahead includes a break with the past. Paul says that before he gave up everything for Jesus, the hologram was

---

2. Cf. LSJ, s.v. "τέλειος."

going well for him personally. He was thriving and had many advantages, at least in the eyes of the world.

> **4** *Though I might also have confidence in the flesh. If any other man thinketh that he hath whereof he might trust in the flesh, I more:* **5** *Circumcised the eighth day, of the stock of Israel, of the tribe of Benjamin, an Hebrew of the Hebrews; as touching the law, a Pharisee;* **6** *Concerning zeal, persecuting the church; touching the righteousness which is in the law, blameless. (Phil 3:4–6)*

Despite all of these perceived benefits, and as confident as he might feel about his situation in the simulation, Paul recognizes that confidence in the flesh—that is, reliance on the things of the world—means nothing. His example is one we can follow with assurance of God's blessing. If we are mature in Christ, we too will recognize the short-lived, even deceitful nature of both our successes and apparent reasons for confidence.

Paul points directly to what matters. Not the simulation itself, but Christ. Our reaching out for Jesus while we are subject to the holographic boundaries around us is essential. It's an intentional movement away from the world's treasures. Stretching out for things before us involves letting go of the world behind us. "For our conversation is in heaven," Paul reminds us (Phil 3:20). KJV's "conversation" is a translation of the word πολίτευμα (*politeuma*), referring to a citizen's rights or citizenship.[3] Recognizing where our true citizenship lies, we should use our time in the hologram to reach out beyond it and to strive for the gain that does not disappear when the simulation ends.

Secular self-confidence commands us to do the opposite. According to worldly teachings, we should not be afraid to embrace whatever we are as we are today, reaching within ourselves for answers. The world tells us to be consumed with the present and to think that we can manipulate or anticipate the future. Confidence in Jesus, however, says to reach out for what lasts forever. It has nothing to do with our own apparent strength. We cannot have confidence in the simulation. It will come to an end. Nevertheless, we can be entirely certain of the One "who shall change our vile body, that it may be fashioned like unto his glorious body, according to the working whereby he is able even to subdue all things unto himself" (Phil 3:21).

---

3. Cf. LSJ, s.v. "πολίτευμα."

D. The Real Role of Faith

Our confidence in Christ is part and parcel of our trust in a faithful God. But what role does faith play in a holographic universe? Unfortunately, many modern Christians already treat faith as its own holographic experience. It is not uncommon to regard faith as nothing more than a simulation. A problem with that approach is that we ignore the hologram's true nature. Our impermanent world is suggestive of a higher reality that initiates or projects the simulation.

If the world is holographic and does suggest the existence of a higher reality, where does faith fit into it? Under the terms of the holographic principle, faith actually plays a very critical role in aligning our focus. Faith fixes our eyes on the reality that lies behind the hologram of our universe. Hebrews 11 clarifies.

> **1** *Now faith is the substance of things hoped for, the evidence of things not seen.* **2** *For by it the elders obtained a good report.* **3** *Through faith we understand that the worlds were framed by the word of God, so that things which are seen were not made of things which do appear.* (Heb 11:1–3)

As seen in the real-life illustrations given in Hebrews 11, faith helps us zoom in on something more permanent than the hologram around us.

In the original Greek text of Hebrews 11:1, the words for "substance" and "evidence" highlight the fact that faith points us toward reality. "Substance" is a translation of ὑπόστασις (*hypostasis*), which literally refers to "standing under" or the act of "supporting." A ὑπόστασις/*hypostasis* is a building's foundation, or the groundwork of a narrative. It is the "substance" because it is the reality or actuality that stands under or supports something. In fact, for this reason, ὑπόστασις/*hypostasis* can be translated as "reality" or "actual existence."[4]

The second half of verse 3 uses similar terminology to account for the reality of "evidence." The Greek word for "evidence" is ἔλεγχος (*elenchos*). It is something that gives the opportunity of refutation, and offers itself for testing and cross-examination. To speak of ἔλεγχος/*elenchos* is to speak of evidence that stands up to scrutiny.

The lesson of Hebrews 11:1–3 is that Christians do not have to be afraid of tests of faith. We don't have to fear questions or challenges. God's Word is truth. How then can we be afraid to investigate it? Others will

---

4. Cf. LSJ, s.v. "ὑπόστασις."

examine it, whether or not we do. Faith is therefore not an act of blindness, but of acting in belief on the evidence of God's faithfulness in the past. Our assurance of God's character and truth rests on the persuasiveness of what God has already faithfully pronounced and accomplished. First Peter 3:15 says that as a believer you should "be ready always to give an answer to every man that asketh you a reason of the hope that is in you with meekness and fear." Having answers about today helps provide us with answers for tomorrow, because once we realize that there is evidence for the truth of the Bible, we have a comprehensive framework for comprehending the present and viewing the future. That is an intellectual, consistent process of faith.

Faith is not about a blind belief in the world as we want it to be. It is about coming to terms with what reality is according to the Bible, and acknowledging the reality that lies beyond the hologram. Hence, we keep our eyes fixed on Jesus, "the author and finisher of our faith" (Heb 12:2). The evidence of God's fulfilled promises and the world around us lead us to realize that this holographic simulation is limited, as we are. Through faith, we have access to increasing knowledge of the higher reality that actually matters, and through faith we invest in a future that is much more than a mere simulation. Living a faith-filled life means living for what lies beyond the hologram and concentrating on the reality behind what we see.

5

The Creator Reaches Out

Lift up your eyes to the heavens, and look upon the earth beneath:
for the heavens shall vanish away like smoke,
and the earth shall wax old like a garment,
and they that dwell therein shall die in like manner:
but my salvation shall be for ever,
and my righteousness shall not be abolished. (Isa 51:6)

A. The Intricacy and Importance of Every Detail

IN HOSEA 12:10, GOD states, "I have also spoken by the prophets, and I have multiplied visions, and used similitudes, by the ministry of the prophets."

The phrase "used similitudes" translates a form of the Hebrew verb הָמָד, *damah*, which means "to be like" or "to resemble." Another way to render the word is "to use comparisons," or similitudes, parables, or symbols.[1] Prophets, visions, and symbols are all means by which God communicates to us. He uses patterns and prophecies to tell us not only about the nature of our world, but what is beyond it.

---

1. Cf. Bible Hub, "1819. damah" (*Strong's Exhaustive Concordance* and *Brown-Driver-Briggs*); and Bible Hub, "'ă·ḏam·meh-." (*Englishman's Concordance*). See also Wilson, "Similitude."

The Bible and the Holographic Universe

Some analogies and parallelisms are more obvious than others, which could be hidden in the tiniest elements of Scripture. Jesus underscores the value of every "jot and tittle" in the Law (Matt 5:18). The jot and tittle are the smallest markings in Hebrew. "Jot" is the transliteration of the Greek word ἰῶτα, *iōta*. *Iota* is the ninth and smallest letter of the Greek alphabet. It is equivalent to *yōd*, the tenth letter of the Hebrew alphabet (modern *yud*).[2] These letters might seem to be the most insignificant letters in their alphabets—and yet they are absolutely essential in the eyes of God Himself. The Name of God in Hebrew even begins with the letter *yod*.[3] A tittle is the small stroke used to distinguish between certain letters of the Hebrew alphabet. Once more, the small size of the mark might make the stroke itself appear unnecessary or meaningless, even though it is necessary for telling letters apart. They cannot be properly written without the tittle.[4] The importance of "jot" and "tittle" is illustrative. Every single mark in Scripture is watched over by God. Given the complexity of every minute detail in Scripture, how could we ever find out the depth of knowledge and wisdom contained in the Bible? ("Canst thou by searching find out God? canst thou find out the Almighty unto perfection?," Job 11:7).

But then, as Peter says, "no prophecy of the scripture is of any private interpretation" (2 Pet 1:20). And Paul states that all Scripture is God-breathed: "given by inspiration of God" (2 Tim 3:16). It is not created by men or designed by humans, but comes straight from God. This is the very meaning of "inspired." The Latin word *inspiro* means "to breathe into": *in* ("in") + *spīrō* ("breathe," "blow"). "Inspired" and "God-breathed" are faithful renderings of the original Greek text of 2 Timothy 3:16, which says that Scripture is θεόπνευστος (*theopneustos*). Θεόπνευστος/*theopneustos* is a compound derived from θεός (*theos*, "God") and πνέω (*pneō*, "blow" or "breathe," in adjectival form "breathed," "blown"). Literally, Scripture is breathed by God.

If we acknowledge that the Bible is in fact inspired by God, our treatment of Scripture should reflect utmost respect and attention to biblical teachings. To say that the Bible is "God-breathed" indicates that it is a divine Source of information. Many people today affirm that they believe in the Bible. Unfortunately, they do not equate that belief with any action or

---

2. Compare Got Questions Ministries, "What Is a Jot?"; and Crowe, "Not One Jot."

3. For more on the Name of God as addressed from a Jewish perspective, see Jewish Virtual Library, "Jewish Concepts."

4. See Easton, "Tittle."

attention to what the Bible says: they do not believe that Scripture presents unchanging, absolute truth. The result is a paradox. It is illogical and impossible to believe that the Bible is the written Word of God, and yet declare that it is merely a compilation of men's personal interpretations with a) limited understanding and b) limited application.

The divine inspiration of Scripture means that every single detail in the Bible is vital. Hosea 12 emphasizes that God works with symbols, patterns, and prophecies, just as is declared by Christ when He states that every jot and tittle of the Mosaic Law is significant. Every element of the Word of God is meaningful and has eternal impact. As God says in Isaiah 55:11: "So shall my word be that goeth forth out of my mouth: it shall not return unto me void, but it shall accomplish that which I please, and it shall prosper in the thing whereto I sent it."

Indeed, every detail in the Bible matters. Therefore every detail indicates something to us about the nature of reality. When we view the information of the universe through the biblical lens, we have the key to accurate interpretation of reality as divinely shown to us by the Author of the universe.

B. Shadows and Copies

The presence of consistent, meaningful patterns deeply embedded throughout the Bible evidences a Single Author working behind the scenes and conveying truth to those who are willing to receive it. The holographic image is structured with analogues to indicate truths about the higher reality. Its order reflects the orderly nature of God: "For God is not the author of confusion, but of peace" (1 Cor 14:33).

The book of Hebrews is an especially apt example of the intricate manner in which the holographic image relates to the outside reality. It affirms that the patterns given in the Old Testament, intricately connected to the revelation of Jesus Christ, are shadows of the higher reality beyond our world. Hebrews further demonstrates the evidence of design shared by the Old and New Testaments. It shows that the Old Testament foreshadows the New, just as the Mosaic Law and priesthood foreshadow Jesus' offices as sacrificial Lamb and High Priest. In these relationships, the transience of our universe becomes clearer, as do our limited perspectives.

The higher reality indicated by the specifics of the Law is no secret. The book of Hebrews repeatedly describes the Tabernacle and prescribed festivals as earthly reflections of heavenly things. Hebrews 8 alludes to the Mosaic Law and its elements as copies intended to point us toward eternal truths. They refer to Jesus the Messiah.

> **4** *For if he were on earth, he should not be a priest, seeing that there are priests that offer gifts according to the law:* **5** *Who serve unto the example and shadow of heavenly things, as Moses was admonished of God when he was about to make the tabernacle: for, See, saith he, that thou make all things according to the pattern shewed to thee in the mount. (Heb 8:4–5)*

Jesus Christ would never serve in the material office of the human priesthood. The Messiah cannot be only a human priest in a material temple. He would be serving in a position that is only a copy of something real. Instead, Jesus is the spiritual High Priest and Atonement. He directly mediates between us and God the Father, who is not limited to this imperfect, passing universe. The priestly duties of Aaron and his sons in the Old Testament, and the Tabernacle where the priests served, were designed to reveal elements of our relationship with God. As Hebrews 9 goes on to explain, the Mosaic Covenant reflected what was to come in the New Covenant.

> **1** *Then verily the first covenant had also ordinances of divine service, and a worldly sanctuary.* **2** *For there was a tabernacle made; the first, wherein was the candlestick, and the table, and the shewbread; which is called the sanctuary.* **3** *And after the second veil, the tabernacle which is called the Holiest of all;* **4** *Which had the golden censer, and the ark of the covenant overlaid round about with gold, wherein was the golden pot that had manna, and Aaron's rod that budded, and the tables of the covenant;* **5** *And over it the cherubims of glory shadowing the mercyseat; of which we cannot now speak particularly.* **6** *Now when these things were thus ordained, the priests went always into the first tabernacle, accomplishing the service of God.* **7** *But into the second went the high priest alone once every year, not without blood, which he offered for himself, and for the errors of the people. (Heb 9:1–7)*

The Holy Spirit has presented wider truths to us through the Tabernacle and Christ's priesthood:

> **8** *The Holy Ghost this signifying, that the way into the holiest of all was not yet made manifest, while as the first tabernacle was yet standing:* **9** *Which was a figure for the time then present, in which were offered both gifts and sacrifices, that could not make him that*

> did the service perfect, as pertaining to the conscience; **10** Which stood only in meats and drinks, and divers washings, and carnal ordinances, imposed on them until the time of reformation. **11** But Christ being come an high priest of good things to come, by a greater and more perfect tabernacle, not made with hands, that is to say, not of this building; **12** Neither by the blood of goats and calves, but by his own blood he entered in once into the holy place, having obtained eternal redemption for us. (Heb 9:8–12)

Later in the same chapter, we are told that the holy places of the Tabernacle are "the figures of the true" (Heb 9:24). Hebrews 10 reiterates that the Mosaic Law has "a shadow of good things to come, and not the very image of the things" (Heb 10:1).

What we see in the Law and Tabernacle is an outline of the real heavenly things. These earthly details are designed to give us a better awareness of realities which we do not comprehend. They are holographic copies of the real things that lie outside of our natural domain.

Time, seasons, and the feasts fit into the same pattern of holographic image and heavenly reality, as Paul says in Colossians 2. He refers to eating, drinking, festivals, new moons, and Sabbaths as "a shadow of things to come," adding, "but the body is of Christ" (Col 2:17).

The word for "shadow" in both Hebrews 8:5 and Colossians 2:17 is σκιά (*skia*). In addition to meaning "shadow," this ancient Greek word also means "reflection" or "phantom." These verses explain that the σκιά/*skia* we live in is a shadow, or a poor reflection of the reality that surrounds us. But what is a reflection or copy if there is no original? A reflection must have something that it is reflecting. Accordingly, the Old Testament Laws and Tabernacle have something that they point us toward: the substance of Christ.

The Bible's terminology is echoed by modern explanations of the holographic universe. In very similar terms, *Discover Magazine* describes the hologram theory as an "unsettling" one in which our universe is "a shadow of the realm where real events take place."[5] A 2017 *Nautilus* article by astrophysicist Brian Koberlein explains that in a holographic universe, "our world of solid objects and three-dimensional space would simply be a shadow of a two-dimensional reality."[6] Cryptographer and cybersecurity specialist Fernando Velázquez cites string theory's suggestion that "our

---

5. Greene, "Our Universe," abstract.
6. Koberlein, "Evidence."

own four-dimensional world is probably only a shadow of some multidimensional universe."[7]

Our world is a "shadow." A shadow of what? Although science is not yet certain, the Bible is. Everything points to the higher reality of the one true God who transcends time and space, and to the Christ whose death and resurrection provide the Atonement desperately needed by humanity. The Mosaic Law and priesthood exemplify the heavenly things and the truth of Jesus.

C. Behind the Veil: Seeing the Throne Room of God

Other biblical pictures of our time and space demonstrate that our universe is more complex and has far more depth and dimensionality than we commonly ascribe to it. Ezekiel and Isaiah's visions are two good examples. Both of these prophets record accounts of encountering God on a different level of reality. The curtain between heaven and earth was pulled back to reveal a tiny part of the splendor of heaven. Reading the prophets' words over two thousand years later, we may find ourselves dismissing and downplaying the sheer wonder of what these men were privileged to see. To be fair, how could we not have a small understanding of and limited appreciation for such amazing sights without having witnessed these visions firsthand? That being said, let's not lose sight of what we can observe from reading. Ezekiel and Isaiah's visions are not dreams or flights of the imagination. What they see and hear is an indication of the awesomeness of God and of the higher reality which Christians will someday share—not because of what the holographic universe is or because of how amazing supernatural reality is, but because of who God is. His glory goes exceedingly beyond all known time and space.

In Isaiah 6, around the late 740s BC, Isaiah tells of seeing "the LORD sitting upon a throne, high and lifted up, and his train filled the temple. Above it stood the seraphims: each one had six wings; with twain he covered his face, and with twain he covered his feet, and with twain he did fly" (Isa 6:1–2). This vision recounts Isaiah's original call to prophetic ministry. In Isaiah 6, a seraph touches Isaiah's lips with a live coal from the altar. "Lo, this hath touched thy lips; and thine iniquity is taken away, and thy sin purged" (Isa 6:7). No human beings other than Isaiah are mentioned in the vision. When he is given such unique access to the Throne of God and the

---

7. Velázquez, "Existence in a Hologram."

seraphim, Isaiah witnesses what the Tabernacle and Temple represent. He is shown the overwhelmingly magnificent reality and holiness of God.

Approximately one hundred and fifty years later, the priest Ezekiel has a similar experience to Isaiah's. "The heavens were opened, and I saw visions of God," he writes, continuing,

> **4** *And I looked, and, behold, a whirlwind came out of the north, a great cloud, and a fire infolding itself, and a brightness was about it, and out of the midst thereof as the colour of amber, out of the midst of the fire.* **5** *Also out of the midst thereof came the likeness of four living creatures.* (Ezek 1:4–5a)

Ezekiel proceeds to describe the cherubim (through verse 25), then God upon the Throne (vv. 26–28).

Ezekiel's encounter truly brings to the fore the distinction between representation and reality. He says that his vision occurs "in the thirtieth year" (Ezek 1:1), 593/592 BC.[8] If he means his own thirtieth year, then Ezekiel is now thirty years old, and has therefore just graduated into priestly service (Num 4:3). Significantly, at thirty, he would only recently be eligible to enter into the Temple to perform priestly duties. Yet Ezekiel lived in the period of the Jews' exile to Babylon. The Temple built by King Solomon had been destroyed less than a decade earlier in 587/586 BC. There was no earthly Temple with a physical Holy Place or Holy of Holies. Therefore, Ezekiel's entry into the priesthood of the Temple is marked instead by entry into the real holy place which the earthly Temple represents: the Throne Room of God. In his vision, Ezekiel skips over the symbolic elements of the sacrificial system. He is taken straight to the heart of the real thing, where God is revealed in unassailable glory.

Isaiah and Ezekiel are fully aware of the reality of their experiences, and they are humbled by these views of God in the Throne Room. Their reports should be humbling for us as well. Consider the majesty of God! His glory is unimaginably magnificent. More than that, these accounts of the supernatural realm also leave us wondering how far the holographic universe extends. Clearly the prophets here see reality. Where is the boundary between the real and the representation? Ezekiel and Isaiah struggle to make sense of the places where the supernatural reaches into the natural. Their style of writing shows that they are simply doing their best to describe sights and sounds beyond human understanding or knowledge. They had

---

8. Grace to You, "Ezekiel."

The Bible and the Holographic Universe

to try to put incredible experiences into language. How could they begin to do the visions justice?

The question is still valid today. The visions of these prophets continue to have more relevance and reality than we encounter in the human world. As scientific knowledge continues to develop, we gain a greater appreciation for the depth of the details in the prophets' accounts. Through their visions, we may have hints of physical properties that still do not make sense to us. Not everything in their visions can be clear to us, given the limitations of human knowledge and perception, of course, and it would be wrong to imply that the things seen by the prophets are merely misunderstood science or natural causes. What we can understand is that the reality they saw was too lofty for them to describe. They had to attempt to convey it to us despite the regular limitations of language and human experience. For instance, as Chuck Missler explains, Ezekiel's vision of the Lord's Chariot Throne in Ezekiel 1 is not an account of a UFO encounter or a dream of modern aircraft, but "a glimpse of a hyperdimensional event."[9] By "hyperdimensional," Missler refers to a human's interaction with dimensions beyond those we readily observe, understand, or inhabit. He reminds his readers that human beings do not live in all known dimensions. Ezekiel is witnessing a hyperdimensional event that is real and cannot be understood as a physical anomaly. Hyperdimensional does not mean not supernatural; it means that Ezekiel was translated outside of the domain we inhabit and interpret.

Moving forward, we can expect that the holographic principle will be used by some to try to debunk the biblical worldview. It would also be easy to be deceived by demonic influences that are able to travel in ways that we can't, or to be conned into thinking that God must be limited by the holographic universe. What we have to understand (as Missler did) is that these two visions offer a small taste of the higher reality, not that they should be used as a means of reducing the supernatural to the natural. God is outside of the program. He is beyond it by definition: the Creator is not bound by the created any more than a human computer programmer is limited by the constraints of a computer game he designs. Of course, our universe is not a game to God. Jesus Christ's suffering and sacrifice far outweigh the importance of any "game." But the truth remains. God made the universal simulation and caused it to begin. He therefore does not have to live within it. He may choose to go in and out of it, but that is the prerogative of the system designer. He can choose to interact with us. His terms dictate the program.

---

9. Missler, *Supplemental Notes*, 10.

The underlying message of these visions, a small sampling of what the Bible has to say about the nature of reality, is unmistakable. Despite how things might appear to us, we do not see the whole of reality. In fact, what we see is nothing greater than a shadow, or a weak image of the heavenly things.

D. The Message of the Bible

Writing from an extremely strong background in information sciences, commentator and teacher Chuck Missler had a rather remarkable way of explaining the Bible. He referred to it as a "collection of sixty-six books . . . written by more than forty authors over several thousands of years, yet we now discover it is an integrated message from outside our time domain."[10]

Hebrews describes the Bible as coming from outside of our known realm as well. God's Word is superhumanly penetrating, incredibly delicate, and eternally relevant:

> *For the word of God is quick, and powerful, and sharper than any twoedged sword, piercing even to the dividing asunder of soul and spirit, and of the joints and marrow, and is a discerner of the thoughts and intents of the heart. (Heb 4:12)*

Ζῶν (*zōn*), the Greek word which reads as "quick" in the KJV, is a participial form of the verb ζάω (*zaō*; or ζῶ, *zō*), "to live." Ζῶν/*zōn* literally means "living." Metaphorically, "to live" can be understood as "to be strong" or "in full life."[11] In English words such as *zoo*-logy or proto-*zoa*, the root *zoo*- indicates "life" or "living thing."

"Powerful" is a translation of the Greek word ἐνεργής (*energēs*), the source for our word "energy." Something that is ἐνεργής/*energēs* is "active" or "effective." The Bible has power because it literally has effect and operates on whatever it touches. Isaiah 55 speaks of the Word of God in very similar terms.

> **10** *For as the rain cometh down, and the snow from heaven, and returneth not thither, but watereth the earth, and maketh it bring forth and bud, that it may give seed to the sower, and bread to the eater:* **11** *So shall my word be that goeth forth out of my mouth: it shall not*

---

10. Missler, "Message." Other helpful resources include Josh McDowell Ministry, "Bible is Unique"; and Ankerberg and Weldon, "What Makes."

11. Cf. LSJ, s.v. "ζῶ."

> *return unto me void, but it shall accomplish that which I please, and it shall prosper in the thing whereto I sent it. (Isa 55:10–11)*

The Word of God never goes anywhere without leaving an impact. It is sharper and more cutting than any sword could ever be. It is divisive, probing, and relentless.

As the incarnation of the Word of the God, Jesus Christ has a comparable effect on human hearts. John 1 explains that Jesus is the glory of God in the flesh.

> *And the Word was made flesh, and dwelt among us, (and we beheld his glory, the glory as of the only begotten of the Father,) full of grace and truth. (John 1:14)*

The Bible and the words (and life) of Jesus Christ cannot help but be divisive. By nature, they are always at work, probing human hearts and souls. Sinful human nature is not comfortable with the truth that God is holy and just. His purity offends us. We as human beings have to reckon with the absolute truth of God's holiness. We are forced to grapple with what God's righteousness reveals to us about reality. Reading the Bible in context and in its fullness convicts us. One way or another, we are faced with its truth.

The exact same dilemma is expressed by Jesus in very stark terms. He presents the ultimate dichotomy. Accept the Messiah or reject the Messiah—and Jesus is the one true Messiah.

> **32** *Whosoever therefore shall confess me before men, him will I confess also before my Father which is in heaven.* **33** *But whosoever shall deny me before men, him will I also deny before my Father which is in heaven.* **34** *Think not that I am come to send peace on earth: I came not to send peace, but a sword.* **35** *For I am come to set a man at variance against his father, and the daughter against her mother, and the daughter in law against her mother in law.* **36** *And a man's foes shall be they of his own household.* **37** *He that loveth father or mother more than me is not worthy of me: and he that loveth son or daughter more than me is not worthy of me.* **38** *And he that taketh not his cross, and followeth after me, is not worthy of me.* **39** *He that findeth his life shall lose it: and he that loseth his life for my sake shall find it. (Matt 10:32–39)*

Jesus is alive and returning to the earth someday in physical form. The Word of God in the form of the Bible is alive and with us today. Because Jesus and the Bible are divine, they confront us with the life and truth of God. We do not have the luxury of interpreting them for ourselves. Although we have the right to decide how we respond to truth, we do not have the ability to redefine or remove the parts we do not like. Truth cannot be altered. The witness of the Word is undeniable, like it or not, and it conveys absolute moral standards.

Fascinatingly, the Bible captures a picture of God's standards in action. The words and deeds of Jesus testify to the holiness of God as a practical exemplar. The Bible and the life of Christ therefore impart to us an enduring account of right and wrong, good and evil, telling us what conduct is acceptable and unacceptable. The message is a living one—not because it is changing or evolving, but because it is eternally constant and relevant. As we grow in Christ through the Holy Spirit, we learn more from reading God's Word. Our ability to discern and understand grows with us. This process does not occur because God or the nature of holiness changes, but rather because we do. Our relationship with Jesus transforms our very essence as it transitions us from impure impermanent beings to pure permanent ones.

As Jesus is unlike any other man, the Bible is unlike any other book. Its scope is not limited to human history or to human nature. Like its Author, the Bible is concerned with the spiritual and eternal. Its focus is on Christ and the story of human redemption.

6

Yearning for Reality

8 *And being found in fashion as a man, he humbled himself,
and became obedient unto death, even the death of the cross.*
9 *Wherefore God also hath highly exalted him,
and given him a name which is above every name:*
10 *That at the name of Jesus every knee should bow, of things in heaven,
and things in earth, and things under the earth. (Phil 2:8–10)*

A. Perspective and Permanency

THE THEORY OF THE holographic universe has a lot to say about the perspective of characters who live inside of a hologram: people inside the hologram do not know what they look like from the outside. What you see isn't always what you get. And with the holographic universe, what we see around us is nothing like what we think it is.

How can we see clearly? Only from a correct external perspective. As dogmatic as it sounds, the biblical worldview is either accurate, or it is not; if it is, then it is the exclusively correct perspective of the universe, and we should use it as our interpretive lens for everything else. Christians recognize the message of the Bible as the correct and fully sufficient lens for orienting our view. The Bible widens our personal point of view. First, so that we are able to incorporate the external universe and spiritual realm into our

Yearning for Reality

worldview; second, so that we may process what is external and realize that there is a proper, meaningful way to understand our position in this world. Most importantly, reading the Bible with an open heart reorients us toward God. It causes us to focus on God, instead of ourselves. The result of building such a connection with the Designer of the universe is a reconciliation with the holographic universe on a macrocosmic level, outside of ourselves, outside of time and space themselves.

We internalize Scripture through reading and memorization. Familiarizing ourselves with the Word of God is a process that helps us to understand why we may never have felt quite at home in this world. Before we are Christians, we belong to the world. It is our home. Nonetheless, we have a yearning for something higher and more meaningful. Our hearts ache to know something enduring and significant. We have a "hole" from the moment we are born.

The term "God-shaped hole" reflects the sentiment captured by the seventeenth-century mathematician and physicist Blaise Pascal. In his fragmentary work *Pensées*, Pascal speaks of human efforts to attain happiness and find goodness.

> What is it then that this desire and this inability proclaim to us, but that there was once in man a true happiness of which there now remain to him only the mark and empty trace, which he in vain tries to fill from all his surroundings, seeking from things absent the help he does not obtain in things present? But these are all inadequate, because the infinite abyss can only be filled by an infinite and immutable object, that is to say, only by God himself.[1]

As Pascal notices, humans inherently seek something beyond ourselves. We are born with a sense of longing. Christians are not the only ones to feel the weight of a human inadequacy and insufficiency. The hole is observed in the secular world as well. In a 2009 interview, actor Shia LaBeouf remarks on "most" actors' tendency to feel unworthy. "I have no idea where this insecurity comes from, but it's a God-sized hole," LaBeouf comments. "If I knew, I'd fill it, and I'd be on my way."[2]

The Bible addresses the origins of this hole. After the fall of man, recorded in Genesis 3, the heart of every human being was corrupted by sin. We continue to have a desire for fulfillment, because we once had fulfillment in a perfect relationship with God. Nothing else can fill the hole that

---

1. Pascal, *Pascal's Pensées*, 113.7, 425.
2. Rader, "Mixed-Up Life."

The Bible and the Holographic Universe

has been created by the gap between perfect God and imperfect humanity.[3] Once we become Christians, the world is no longer our home, and God has filled that hole in our hearts. He has brought us life. No wonder the world feels so incompatible with our new hearts! It is old and broken. The world is still under the curse. We are not. We are new and made whole. In *Mere Christianity*, C. S. Lewis summarizes, "If I find in myself a desire which no experience in this world can satisfy, the most probable explanation is that I was made for another world."[4]

Every human soul is made for an eternal destination outside of the hologram. In that sense, the world is nobody's home. Those who reject God are merely dwelling on the earth until they enter into eternity (for examples of unbelievers as being called "earth-dwellers," or "those who inhabit the earth," see Luke 24:35 and Revelation 6:10, 8:13, and 11:10, among others). Every single human being is on a journey to either heaven or to hell. As C. S. Lewis says in reference to the end of each individual soul's journey:

> There are no *ordinary* people. You have never talked to a mere mortal. Nations, cultures, arts, civilization—these are mortal, and their life is to ours as the life of a gnat. But it is immortals whom we joke with, work with, marry, snub, and exploit—immortal horrors or everlasting splendours.[5]

For Christians, Hebrews 11 illustrates our search for another country or homeland. Abel, Enoch, Noah, Abraham, Sarah, and others are examples of those who have gone before us in the search.

> 13 *These all died in faith, not having received the promises, but having seen them afar off, and were persuaded of them, and embraced them, and confessed that they were strangers and pilgrims on the earth.* 14 *For they that say such things declare plainly that they seek a country.* 15 *And truly, if they had been mindful of that country from whence they came out, they might have had opportunity to have returned.* 16 *But now they desire a better country, that is, an heavenly: wherefore God is not ashamed to be called their God: for he hath prepared for them a city.* (Heb 11:13–16)

The examples of such heroes of the faith matter for us not merely because these people sought for another homeland and fought against all odds to

---

3. See Got Questions Ministries, "Does Everyone."
4. Lewis, *Mere Christianity*, 121.
5. Lewis, *Weight of Glory*, 15.

obtain it, but because they found its sole guaranteed Provider. They did not earn entry into eternal life. It was given to them by faith, just as it is to us.

> **39** *And these all, having obtained a good report through faith, received not the promise:* **40** *God having provided some better thing for us, that they without us should not be made perfect. (Heb 11:39-40)*

These believers of the past stood out among the people of the world. They are known as heroes of the faith because they were incompatible with those who were around them, that is, with those who did not seek and find the one true God. In antiquity, as today, believers and unbelievers do not share the same goals.

Each human soul is undergoing a constant search for a deeper and higher reality. On some level, we instinctively know that the world around us is not all there is. If we had the ability to see more perceptively, or perhaps to think more clearly, it would become apparent how transient and empty the holographic image is on its own. The realization of the image's impermanence touches every soul. In the end, it drives us in one of two directions: into the arms of Christ, or into an embrace of the insanity that is sin. Strange as it seems, the human race is already naturally and literally insane due to our fallen nature. The light of God is our hope. He is the only way we can regain sanity lost at the fall in Genesis 3. Such hope is scandalizing to our human sensibilities. The Rock of Offense (1 Pet 2:8), Christ, is the one opportunity for a firm foundation. This One, the Son of Man, the Messiah, stabilizes our hearts and minds on a solid and sane awareness of true reality.

B. Living in Tents of the Body

The Bible frequently refers to our temporary habitation on Earth as a "tent" or a temporary dwelling place. Second Corinthians 5 says,

> **1** *For we know that if our earthly house of this tabernacle were dissolved, we have a building of God, an house not made with hands, eternal in the heavens.* **2** *For in this we groan, earnestly desiring to be clothed upon with our house which is from heaven:* **3** *If so be that being clothed we shall not be found naked.* **4** *For we that are in this tabernacle do groan, being burdened: not for that we would be unclothed, but clothed upon, that mortality might be swallowed up of life. (2 Cor 5:1-4)*

The Bible and the Holographic Universe

"Tabernacle" in the KJV is the translation for the word σκῆνος (*skēnos*), meaning "tent" or "hut."[6] In 2 Peter 1:13–14, Peter speaks of his body as a "tabernacle," σκήνωμα (*skēnōma*, "quarters"). Σκήνωμα/*skēnōma* is related to σκηνέω (*skēneō*), the same verb to which σκῆνος/*skēnos* is related. Σκηνέω/*skēneō* means "to dwell in a tent," "encamp," or "to be quartered."[7] Our bodies are compared to temporary encampments and tents.

Although less apparent in the English, humans' temporary tent-living in the world is reflected in the language of John 1. Here, however, the concept at first might seem out of place. John has spent the first half of the chapter, the very beginning of his Gospel, speaking of eternal things. His book has begun with an eternal genealogy: that of Jesus Christ, the Word of God. But what looks out of place only demonstrates the grace of God through the comparison. John is making a sharp contrast between the eternality of the Word, without any beginning or end, and the ignorant instability of humanity, on its own doomed to the ravages of willful sin. The Word looks out of place because of the incredible paradox of finding perfect God among imperfect human beings. The paradox is further heightened by the fact that humanity belongs to the Lord, and yet refuses to recognize the truth of its own origins: the Word "came unto his own, and his own received him not" (John 1:11).

In the midst of the distinction between God's eternal nature and humans' sinful nature, John underscores the stunning love of God. Such love can bridge the gap between temporary and eternal, and does it by choice. The Word made a deliberate choice to enter into the world of temporary tents and tabernacles:

> *And the Word was made flesh, and dwelt among us, (and we beheld his glory, the glory as of the only begotten of the Father,) full of grace and truth. (John 1:14)*

The amazing declaration of God's love rests on the divine decision to take on a transient covering in the transient human world. John is referring to Jesus, the incarnate Word of God, and is reassuring all people who will receive the good news: it is no accident that Jesus dwelt on the earth.

The word "dwelt" in John 1:14 is a translation of ἐσκήνωσεν (*eskēnōsen*), from the verb σκηνόω (*skēnoō*): "to pitch tent(s)," "encamp," or "dwell." Since this verb is the action of living in a tent or making one's encampment, it

---

6. Cf. LSJ, s.v. "σκῆνος."
7. Cf. LSJ, s.v. "σκηνέω."

can simply mean "to take up (one's) abode."[8] The living Word of God, Jesus, "tented" among us. He pitched a tent and encamped here. His own creation has the utter privilege of God's presence. As John 1 shows, it is an expression of the ultimate sacrifice that God would don a human body, be born on Earth, live a life in a sinful and imperfect world, and endure a horrendous and humiliating death, all the while unrecognized.

While the description of the body as a dwelling is not unusual, the consistent biblical worldview toward habitations and a suggestively holographic universe is unique. Secular authors prior to the writings of the Gospels had already compared the human body to a dwelling-place for the spirit or soul. The physician Hippocrates, philosophers Democritus and Plato, and others had used this type of terminology centuries earlier.[9] For Christians, the most pressing aspect of the idea of the body as a tent is that the tent does not last. The tent is an impermanent home. It is a dwelling-place that can be "destroyed" (or "dissolved," "brought to an end"[10]), as Paul says in 2 Corinthians 5:1.[11] Christianity alone has a viable solution to the problem of such vulnerability. The good news of Jesus Christ is that a permanent, eternal abiding with God is available right now, in an age of grace, and that every living human being has the opportunity to choose a lasting dwelling-place of perfection and abundant life.

The emphatic contrast of "eternal" vs. "temporary" also stands out in Luke 16. There, Jesus instructs us to use our worldly resources wisely:

> And I say unto you, Make to yourselves friends of the mammon of unrighteousness; that, when ye fail, they may receive you into everlasting habitations. (Luke 16:9)

A "habitation" is a place where someone dwells. Here, "habitations" is a translation of σκηνάς (skēnas), from σκηνή (skēnē). Σκηνή/skēnē is another word for "tent" or "tabernacle."[12] In the Greek, σκηνάς/skēnas is modified by the adjective αἰωνίους (aiōnious), "eternal," "everlasting."[13]

---

8. Cf. LSJ, s.v. "σκηνόω."

9. Occurrences are listed in LSJ, s.v. "σκῆνος."

10. The Greek term is καταλυθῇ, literally referring to an action of breaking up, dissolving, or unloosing (cf. LSJ, s.v. "καταλύω").

11. See further entries on 2 Corinthians 5 in Ellicott, *Ellicott's Commentary*.

12. Cf. LSJ, s.v. "σκηνή."

13. Cf. LSJ, s.v. "αἰώνιος."

Right now, we are simply pilgrims and sojourners on the earth. Like nomads living in tents, we move from place to place here. Our true eternal bodies are not inside of the holographic image because they are images or shadows. They are real and eternal. For those who follow Christ, they are bodies of eternal life and perfect health. For those who reject Jesus, the eternal body is one of death and decay, "for their worm shall not die, neither shall their fire be quenched" (Isa 66:24b).

Temporary tents may be useful for a time, but they wear out. They are not designed to be permanent homes. So, too, are our bodies not designed to be permanent. We are dwelling in short-term tents. And while our tents are fine for the short time that we live on the earth, we can't take them with us. If we belong to Christ, then we shouldn't even want to keep them forever. These tents are temporary. Like the rest of the image, they are fading. The permanent is yet to come. That is why the adjective in Luke 16:9 is critical: the habitations or dwellings in our future are not the normal, temporary, and transient types of tents we inhabit now. They are just the opposite: eternal, everlasting, and ongoing. They are for forever.

C. Investing in the Future

If we are entities of information living in a non-permanent place, how do we plan ahead for the permanent world that is coming? Paul tells us that everything we do will be tested by God in fire. "Every man's work shall be made manifest" (1 Cor 3:13a). Even though we are saved, we could find that we have wasted time focusing on treasures that do not last into eternity.

> *14 If any man's work abide which he hath built thereupon, he shall receive a reward. 15 If any man's work shall be burned, he shall suffer loss: but he himself shall be saved; yet so as by fire. (1 Cor 3:14–15)*

In Matthew 6, Jesus says,

> *19 Lay not up for yourselves treasures upon earth, where moth and rust doth corrupt, and where thieves break through and steal: 20 But lay up for yourselves treasures in heaven, where neither moth nor rust doth corrupt, and where thieves do not break through nor steal: 21 For where your treasure is, there will your heart be also. (Matt 6:19–21)*

Once we realize that the present world is a hologram, or at the very least a place that is passing away, it becomes increasingly obvious that apparent gains of "today" do not matter for "tomorrow." "For we brought nothing into this world, and it is certain we can carry nothing out" (1 Tim 6:7). The world tries to understand true success as material profit or our ability to avoid offending other people. The truth is, though, that however much we prosper or get along with others, our lives are not intended to be focused on this present age. As Jesus puts it, "For what shall it profit a man, if he shall gain the whole world, and lose his own soul?" (Mark 8:36).

First, we invest in eternity by placing our faith in Christ. Without Jesus, we cannot even begin to make any positive investments for the future. Prior to salvation, we are caught in overwhelming sin:

> *But we are all as an unclean thing, and all our righteousnesses are as filthy rags; and we all do fade as a leaf; and our iniquities, like the wind, have taken us away. (Isa 64:6)*

Isaiah was speaking long before Jesus walked the earth. He understood the need for the Messiah. This is why the whole chapter of Isaiah 64 expresses a deep longing for God's mercy. Nor is Isaiah restricting his declaration to the Jewish people. He alludes to the situation that has been "since the beginning of the world" (Isa 64:4a). Someone who could be perfect and righteous would indeed be investing in the future beyond our world, because that person would merit God's favor. Unfortunately, as fallen creatures, we are inevitably part of the hologram and its system of decay. We continuously choose to act in sin and unrighteousness. "And there is none that calleth upon thy name," Isaiah cries (Isa 64:7a).

Through the prophet Jeremiah, the Lord pronounces that all of human experience and profit are nothing.

> **23** *Thus saith the Lord, Let not the wise man glory in his wisdom, neither let the mighty man glory in his might, let not the rich man glory in his riches:* **24** *But let him that glorieth glory in this, that he understandeth and knoweth me, that I am the Lord which exercise lovingkindness, judgment, and righteousness, in the earth: for in these things I delight, saith the Lord. (Jer 9:23–24)*

We might say that, in the long run, worldly profit on worldly terms turns out to be a "non-profit" venture! A relationship with God is the only thing of which anyone can rightly boast. Wisdom, wealth, and strength offer no eternal security, however much we may try to find significance or safety through them. And as with Isaiah 64, Jeremiah 9 shows that the curse of sin prevents humans from choosing righteousness, much less practicing it.

The Bible and the Holographic Universe

> ³ *And they bend their tongues like their bow for lies: but they are not valiant for the truth upon the earth; for they proceed from evil to evil, and they know not me, saith the Lord.* ⁴ *Take ye heed every one of his neighbour, and trust ye not in any brother: for every brother will utterly supplant, and every neighbour will walk with slanders.* ⁵ *And they will deceive every one his neighbour, and will not speak the truth: they have taught their tongue to speak lies, and weary themselves to commit iniquity. (Jer 9:3–5)*

"Through deceit they refuse to know me," the Lord adds (Jer 9:6b). Instead of being obedient and following God, the people "have walked after the imagination of their own heart" and committed idolatry (Jer 9:14). They willfully chose sin, and sin continued to misalign their focus. The same truth remains for us: sin perverts our view of both today and eternity.

Second, we invest by rejecting evil and pursuing righteousness, godliness, faith, love, patience, and gentleness (1 Tim 6:11). As our character changes, we become more like Christ, and bear fruit that honors God and affects others for good. Just as Jeremiah 9:23 condemns self-glorification through resources and wisdom alone, Jeremiah 9:24 demonstrates that a relationship with God does have actual worth. However, such worth is found in God's glory and value connected to absolute holiness; that is, to God's "lovingkindness, judgment, and righteousness." These are not transient qualities. They are directly linked to the absolute standard of goodness inherent in God's own nature. "For in these things I delight, saith the Lord" (Jer 9:24b). All of these characteristics reflect the importance of having a proper approach toward eternal values. On the one hand, no sinful human can invest in them without having a relationship with Christ, and thus being able to invest in the first place; and on the other, these are the eternal investments that are worth pursuing, and they have intrinsic positive value.

When Paul admonishes the rich to "do good" in order to "be rich in good works," he shows us more of what a good foundation for the future looks like (1 Tim 6:18–19). Even doing good works toward our enemies is an investment toward eternity once we are saved (Luke 6:35). Spreading the Gospel is an investment as well: not only do we contribute to our own spiritual "bank account" by doing good and speaking love, but we are also helping others to see how they can have an "account" of their own (see Jude 22–23).

A final word on rewards, treasures, and eternal securities is Jesus' direct instruction in Matthew 6:

But seek ye first the kingdom of God, and his righteousness; and all these things shall be added unto you. (Matt 6:33)

Investment for the future starts and ends with Christ. From accepting salvation to doing good works so that others can see the love of Jesus, all that we put into the future is dependent on Jesus. The hologram will end in a moment. When it disappears, will it take the fruit of your time, money, and efforts with it?

D. The Origins of Jesus Christ

When we place our future in the hands of Christ, we are making a sound investment in eternity. No man has ever made a greater impact on the world than Jesus of Nazareth. Ostensibly a simple Jewish carpenter born to a humble man and his young wife, Jesus is the only man to enter the universe willingly and with awareness of the true reality. Jesus' life, death, and resurrection are the embodiment of the Creator's reaching out to us from beyond our known world.

Every Christmas season, over 160 countries officially commemorate the birth of Jesus Christ.[14] As of 2010, around 2.2 billion people identified as Christian.[15] In 2013, a software algorithm that analyzes internet searches found that Jesus is the "most famous person in history," followed by Napoleon in second place, and then by Mohammad in third.[16] Jesus Christ's fame is predicted to endure as second to none.

What is it about Jesus that has so thoroughly turned the world upside down? He was condemned by the Pharisees and Sadducees. He clearly would have been forgotten by time or forever derided as a blasphemer if the religious leaders of the first century AD had had their way. He was never accepted by the world. He would have been welcomed as a magician or an entertaining diversion by civic leaders, but not as a life-changing revealer of hearts and motives. He was rejected by the Jews. He would have been a nuisance to the Romans.

His origin is what makes Jesus utterly unique. With a divine identity backed up by divine credentials, Jesus Christ is far more than a mere mortal

---

14. World Population Review, "Countries."

15. The Pew Research Center estimates that the Muslim population will exceed the number of Christians by 2070, likely with roughly equal numbers of Muslims and Christians by 2050 (Chappell, "World's Muslim Population").

16. Daily Mail, "How Jesus."

man. He was the first and only human to come from outside the hologram. He could, did, and does have a claim to being an essential part of the hologram's creation. While the rest of us are part of the creation, Jesus is the Christ, the living Word, the Creator.

Shown to be the long-awaited Messiah, Jesus demonstrated a complete separation from any of the limitations that govern our holographic universe. He was and is in no way bound by the natural laws of the holographic image. Boundaries of time and space have no hold over God. He is unchanging. As emphasized by Old Testament and New Testament prophecies, Jesus the Christ has always been and will always be. In an awesome pronouncement about the origins of the Messiah, Micah 5:2 states that the Christ's "goings forth have been from of old, from everlasting." Jesus' origins are from everlasting. He is eternal and never has a beginning or end.

Jesus' origin raised controversy among the Jews in a conversation regarding Abraham, as recorded in John 8. Jesus asserted a personal timelessness by drawing an important contrast. His word would prevent those who believed it from experiencing (lasting and eternal) death (John 8:51). The Jews, incensed that a man would dare to make such a declaration, challenged the claim immediately.

> **52** *Then said the Jews unto him, Now we know that thou hast a devil. Abraham is dead, and the prophets; and thou sayest, If a man keep my saying, he shall never taste of death.* **53** *Art thou greater than our father Abraham, which is dead? and the prophets are dead: whom makest thou thyself? (John 8:52–53)*

A mortal man who experiences time in a linear way and who is limited by the boundaries of a holographic universe could never have successfully denied the power of death. Thankfully, Jesus was no mere mortal man. He answered with the confident assurance of an intimate oneness with God.

> **54** *Jesus answered, If I honour myself, my honour is nothing: it is my Father that honoureth me; of whom ye say, that he is your God:* **55** *Yet ye have not known him; but I know him: and if I should say, I know him not, I shall be a liar like unto you: but I know him, and keep his saying.* **56** *Your father Abraham rejoiced to see my day: and he saw it, and was glad.* **57** *Then said the Jews unto him, Thou art not yet fifty years old, and hast thou seen Abraham?* **58** *Jesus said unto them, Verily, verily, I say unto you, Before Abraham was, I am. (John 8:54–58)*

Yearning for Reality

Jesus' statement in this passage is a direct answer to the charge of *claiming* to be divine or untouched by time. He employs the sacred Name of God in John 8:58. The Jews are outraged that Jesus would invoke any comparison with God. In response, Jesus does not placate them. He instead speaks very clearly. "I AM" is the personal name God cited in Exodus 3, when preparing to send Moses back to Egypt for the deliverance of the enslaved Israelites.

> 14 *And God said unto Moses, I Am That I Am: and he said, Thus shalt thou say unto the children of Israel, I Am hath sent me unto you.* 15 *And God said moreover unto Moses, Thus shalt thou say unto the children of Israel, the Lord God of your fathers, the God of Abraham, the God of Isaac, and the God of Jacob, hath sent me unto you: this is my name for ever, and this is my memorial unto all generations. (Exod 3:14–15)*

"This is my memorial," God says. When Jesus openly assumes God's Name in John 8, the Jews who hear recognize the reference. They see that Jesus is claiming to be the Messiah. He is claiming to be God—and for that, they furiously attempt to take retaliation.

> *Then took they up stones to cast at him: but Jesus hid himself, and went out of the temple, going through the midst of them, and so passed by. (John 8:59)*

If the Christ was to be one with God, then the Christ was to be outside of the repercussions of time and decay. His angry crowd of listeners realized this. If Jesus saw Abraham, Jesus was no ordinary young man of the first century. And if Jesus was the I AM, Jesus was One with God. In our terms, Jesus was outside of the holographic image, because the Christ is not limited by any temporary or human boundaries. The very idea that Jesus might claim to be the Christ was enough to infuriate the disbelieving listeners.

John 1 is one of the most familiar passages when it comes to the Godhead and Jesus' identity as the living Word of God. Here we read that Jesus existed eternally. Before the beginning of the hologram, *Jesus is.* Creation itself was dependent on the Word from before the moment of the world's inception.

> 1 *In the beginning was the Word, and the Word was with God, and the Word was God.* 2 *The same was in the beginning with God.* 3 *All things were made by him; and without him was not any thing made that was made. (John 1:1–3)*

The Bible and the Holographic Universe

In Revelation 22:13, Jesus identifies as "Alpha and the Omega, the beginning and the end, the first and the last." Thankfully, Jesus' interaction in the flesh with those who are inside the hologram is far from complete. Jesus *was* before the beginning of the simulation, *is* today, and *will be* there before it ends. He is the definitive Beginning and the End. The entire simulation, as well as everything that we cannot see in existence around it, depends on Jesus Christ.

7

Time and Knowledge

No man can come to me, except the Father which hath sent me draw him: and I will raise him up at the last day. (John 6:44)

A. The Universe, in 2D and 3D (and 4D)

THE WHOLE POINT OF the holographic principle is that all of the information contained inside an object is visible on the object's surface. Since the entire object is made of bits of information, then theoretically, someone looking at the object from the outside sees the whole object at once.

In our case, the universe is the object. From the outside, it is a two-dimensional projection. Its information is all spread out so to be seen at the same time. The shape and depth of our world appear three-dimensional from the inside, but only because we are on the inside. Meanwhile, outside, everything looks flat. Time itself is entirely visible. Professor Kostas Skenderis (University of Southampton) has compared the idea to regular holograms, like the kind encoded in a flat credit card. A three-dimensional image is contained on a two-dimensional surface. In the entertainment industry, 3D movies offer another example. These movies are featured and contained on a flat screen, and do not have any actual shape or depth. However, viewers can experience false shape and depth while viewing a 3D movie because of the illusionary technology used to shoot the original images. A holographic universe takes the same idea a step further. Inhabiting illusory bodies, we are living inside an illusionary three-dimensional world with apparent objects that we can touch, pick up, handle, or transport.[1]

Comparing the world to a 3D movie is an interesting approach, except that it doesn't quite incorporate the immediacy of how the holographic image could feel to someone inside it. Someone watching a movie does not necessarily get caught up in the emotions and suspense as thoroughly as does a character living through the plot of the movie. Our natural situation is closer to that of the immersed character than an outside viewer. To us, days appear to come one after another. Each day presents its own uncertainty and its own worries. Every day brings decisions and dilemmas. Since we do not see the whole picture, we make our decisions based on the best information available to us at the time. Still, however well we plan or prepare, we never know what tomorrow will bring on this earth. Outcomes can be completely unexpected.

That isn't to say that life does not have meaning. Everything we experience is real. In their own ways, every day and every decision have eternal impact, even if we don't see how things fit together or what the impact will look like a million years from now. Living with that awareness of tomorrow transforms our perspective, giving us a million-year mindset instead of a moment-by-moment one.

But we are still trapped within the holographic image. Our limitations confine us. We live in the moment of what is happening. In fact, instead of thinking of ourselves like characters in a movie, it might be easier to conceive of the holographic principle as a way of showing how we are like characters in a book. Characters inside a book are caught inside a two-dimensional world. The pages of the book are flat. The words and letters forming the sentences of the story are (basically) flat. But to the characters, their world is vibrant, alive, and suspenseful. It is full of shapes and contours.

By contrast, a reader can open the book to the beginning and end at the same time. He can choose to see the ending at any time and never has to be surprised by any outcome. To some extent, by using imagination or writing a different ending, he can engage with the story like a two-dimensional character might. He can imagine how the story would seem to someone who lives inside of it.

---

1. The analogy and the comparison to 3D movies as described by Skenderis are explored by Beall, "Theory Claims." The technology used to produce and view 3D movies is explored by Ayyar, "Understanding the Technology."

Time and Knowledge

This is a useful analogy for how we approach the holographic image, even though the best analogy does not begin to do justice to God's role. He is no mere reader of a storybook. The Lord does not put one finger in the front of the book and another finger in the end in order to see multiple parts at the same time. Instead, to God, the entire book is always visible.

Even better than a book, then, is probably the analogy of a bubble. Think of all of human history as a clear gigantic bubble, like the type blown by children playing outside on a summer day. We live on the surface of the bubble. Every human being's experience is like one little point on a gigantic circular sphere that is transparent and fragile. (This is not an argument that humans are all connected or that we have some kind of a "hive mind," but an analogy for explaining how space and time might look from outside of a holographic image.) The bubble is the entire spacetime of human history. God sees every bit of the bubble at once. He created it, sees through it, and can view all of it simultaneously. A tiny atom that is part of a tiny speck somewhere on one part of the surface of the bubble does not "see" what is happening elsewhere on the bubble. If all of spacetime is a transparent sphere like a bubble, it will pop someday, leaving only the world into which it came. Temporary and flimsy, the bubble can't and won't last.

Unlike characters in most movies or books, however, and unlike any speck on the surface of a bubble, we have a unique advantage. If left to ourselves, our view would be mostly restricted to the three-dimensional world. Yet we are not left to ourselves. The Bible with its divine authority offers a glimpse into the two-dimensional reality of the universe. To God, outside of the 3D constraints of our perspective, all of the universe's information is equally visible and available. God tells us about it in the Bible. He gives us access to an understanding that we could never hope to have on our own.

B. The Nature of Time (God Knows What You Chose)

The fact that God sees all of the universe at once, with all of its bits of information distinctly clear and perfectly complete, helps to make sense of the higher viewpoint that is so graciously shared with us in the Bible. He sees time differently than we do. Time is not something that God needs or uses.

Right now, as you read the words on this page, you are perceiving of time as a linear concept. One second comes after another. You understand time past as "history," and look ahead to what will come in the "future." The seconds on your clock, whether digital or analog, are ticking away. "Time

The Bible and the Holographic Universe

marches on," "a race against time," "before (or after) one's time," "time flies." These phrases and others capture our idea of time as something that moves forward with one second, minute, or hour coming after another.

But time is only a measurement that enables humans to understand the decay of the fallen universe around us. When sin entered the world, the corrupted universe began its decline. Just as it had a starting point, it also has an end that is coming. God sees the start and finish all at once. He sees all of the universe's information simultaneously. He sees the past, present, and future. They are all clear before the face of their timeless Creator, as if they are written neatly on the flat surface of a piece of paper.

Physicists have increasingly conceived of time as a construct or conceptual framework. In a 1955 letter, Albert Einstein remarked, "For us devout physicists, the distinction between past, present, and future has merely the significance of an illusion, even if a persistent one."[2]

In other words, time is just a way for us to think about the world around us. According to physicist Lee Smolin, "Relativity strongly suggests that the whole history of the world is a timeless unity; past, present, and future have no meaning apart from human subjectivity."[3] Smolin's statement indicates that time is a means of interpretation. However, his view of time does not look beyond the reality of time as a subjective measurement that humans use to make better sense of our world. Smolin argues that time is the most foundational feature of reality, and that there is nothing that is separate from time.

From a Christian perspective, the subjectivity of time exactly fits humans' small understanding of God's nature. The holographic principle upholds the idea that something is outside of time as we understand it. Time can be both unified (because God sees all of it at once, and only those subject to time see it as linear moments of past, present, and future) and illusory (because time is not fundamental to God's view of the universe, and time is created for human beings). This same awareness of time is promoted in the Bible. Everything we are told about God, everything we infer from creation, and everything that we logically conclude about what God must be—all of these things point to the timelessness of the Lord. Everything

---

2. "Für uns gläubige Physiker hat die Scheidung zwischen Vergangenheit, Gegenwart und Zukunft nur die Bedeutung einer, wenn auch hartnäckigen, Illusion" (my translation). Quoted From Einstein's March 21, 1955, letter to Vero and Bice Besso. Text cited by Jammer, *Concepts*, 239 (as quoted from Speziali, *Albert Einstein, Michele Besso*, 537–38).

3. Smolin, *Time Reborn*, xxii. Cf. Moskowitz, "Controversially."

shows that time is not eternal, and everything shows that God does not depend upon the passing of time.

Engineers may note that time has an objectivity to it as well, because time can be measured outside of personal experience. Time is subjective in that it is a construct related to human experience; it is objective in that the time on a clock does not reflect an individual person's "feelings" or "impressions" about "what time it is." Yet whatever else it is, time is a measurement designed for our benefit as human beings. Humans need time. God does not. We are bound by it. He is not. "My times are in thy hand," David says (Ps 31:15a), realizing that God has full awareness of time. Peter writes, "But, beloved, be not ignorant of this one thing, that one day is with the Lord as a thousand years, and a thousand years as one day" (2 Pet 3:8).

Perception of time leads to an interesting point that has troubled Christians for centuries and caused division within the church. Do humans have free will or is our eternal destiny a matter of predestination? Do we choose Jesus Christ of our own volition? Or are we chosen for salvation, fated to be saved because of divine selection?

Consider the following verses:

Free Will:[4]

> *But as many as received him, to them gave he power to become the sons of God, even to them that believe on his name. (John 1:12)*
>
> *If ye love me, keep my commandments. (John 14:15)*
>
> *For, brethren, ye have been called unto liberty; only use not liberty for an occasion to the flesh, but by love serve one another. (Gal 5:13)*
>
> *13 Let no man say when he is tempted, I am tempted of God: for God cannot be tempted with evil, neither tempteth he any man: 14 But every man is tempted, when he is drawn away of his own lust, and enticed. 15 Then when lust hath conceived, it bringeth forth sin: and sin, when it is finished, bringeth forth death. (Jas 1:13–15)*
>
> *The Lord is not slack concerning his promise, as some men count slackness; but is longsuffering to us-ward, not willing that any should perish, but that all should come to repentance. (2 Pet 3:9)*

---

4. Free will and Arminianism are contrasted by Marlowe, "What Is Arminianism?"

The Bible and the Holographic Universe

And he is the propitiation for our sins: and not for ours only, but also for the sins of the whole world. (1 John 2:2)

[19] *And hereby we know that we are of the truth, and shall assure our hearts before him.* [20] *For if our heart condemn us, God is greater than our heart, and knoweth all things. (1 John 3:19–20)*

Predestination:

Before I formed thee in the belly I knew thee; and before thou camest forth out of the womb I sanctified thee, and I ordained thee a prophet unto the nations. (Jer 1:5)

Ye have not chosen me, but I have chosen you, and ordained you, that ye should go and bring forth fruit, and that your fruit should remain: that whatsoever ye shall ask of the Father in my name, he may give it you. (John 15:16)

Moreover whom he did predestinate, them he also called: and whom he called, them he also justified: and whom he justified, them he also glorified. (Rom 8:30)

(For the children being not yet born, neither having done any good or evil, that the purpose of God according to election might stand, not of works, but of him that calleth;) (Rom 9:11)

According as he hath chosen us in him before the foundation of the world, that we should be holy and without blame before him in love. (Eph 1:4)

[11] *In whom also we have obtained an inheritance, being predestinated according to the purpose of him who worketh all things after the counsel of his own will:* [12] *That we should be to the praise of his glory, who first trusted in Christ. (Eph 1:11–12)*

Who hath saved us, and called us with an holy calling, not according to our works, but according to his own purpose and grace, which was given us in Christ Jesus before the world began. (2 Tim 1:9)

To some, these passages have appeared contradictory, or led to seemingly irreconcilable ideas about God. "Free will" is generally used to refer to humans' individual decisions to accept Jesus as Lord. "Predestination," by contrast, is typically regarded as the idea that God predetermines who

Time and Knowledge

will be able to accept Jesus. How can the two co-exist? Do we choose, or does God?

Elements of both apparently can be true. As some commentators have noted, free will and predestination are not as incompatible as they might appear. We can have the ability to make choices freely even if God practices predestination in our lives. "God predestines in and through our choices because God is all-knowing and all-powerful," remarks apologist Matt Slick. Slick uses the illustration of arranging for his child to choose to eat ice cream rather than something else. He can offer the child either a bowl of ice cream or a bowl of rocks. Even though the father knows which choice the child will make, the child does have free will. The fact that the father knows what the child will do does not affect or hamper the child's ability to make the choice. The child maintains free will.[5]

Who chooses whom in the situation of free will and predestination? The answer appears to go in both directions. We choose God. He chooses us. "A person really believes in Christ," states author Fritz Chery, "and that is an act of his will. He willingly comes to Jesus. And yes, God predestined all who come to Jesus by faith."[6]

One system of biblical interpretation that approaches the approximation of holographic temporality and information is Molinism. Although not all Molinists have the same ideas about the nature of God's knowledge, an underlying tenet of Molinism is that God is sovereign, and yet people have a libertarian free will. Molinism affirms that God possesses "middle knowledge." He understands every single contingent world and every single contingent choice that every single individual creature could or would ever make. Molinism operates under the acceptance of contrafactuals, or counterfactuals. Contrafactuals are the scenarios that express and explore what "would be" or "would have been" if something had (or had not) happened, or were (or were not) happening now. The contrafactuals and contingents of our world form a basis for the Molinist view: God knows what everyone would have done if every other circumstance had happened.

Like every other system of thought, Molinism relies on human awareness of time, simply because human vocabulary and conceptions of time limit our comprehension of God's interaction with "time." Many Molinists maintain that God actualized a particular universe due to a supreme,

---

5. Slick, "If Predestination Is True." See Got Questions Ministries, "Predestination vs. Free Will"; and Deem, "Predestination vs. Free Will."

6. Chery, "Predestination vs. Free Will."

The Bible and the Holographic Universe

intricate knowledge of every universe. Knowing every single contingency, God made real or brought about a particular universe among all of the possible worlds.

A version of Molinism could very well represent the most specific expression of converging elements of predestination and free will. A drawback to some descriptions of God's middle knowledge in Molinism, however, is that they can imply an actualization process that qualifies God, as if the Lord is subject to the time constraints of knowing events *before* and actualizing them *after* acquiring foreknowledge, whereas God is completely outside of time. But this objection may be easily enough answered with the point that even speaking of creation as a *moment* of God's speaking the world into existence represents a reference to time, and God is outside of time. This is not necessarily an issue of the logic behind Molinism so much as it is the restrictions of human language and understanding.

Molinism depends on God's logical awareness of every contingency, instead of a temporal knowledge that develops over time. Thus, Molinism might best explore the implications of God's foreknowledge and our choice, even as its attempt to navigate unreality and reality display a recurring problem of human boundaries: our interpretation and comprehension of time, conveyed through the limitations of language, repeatedly have recourse to space and time.[7] As humans, we cannot really conceptualize reality without thinking in terms of both space and time.

Ultimately, under the terms of the holographic principle, predestination and free will are not at odds with each other. To God, the information that comprises our universe is completely visible. He sees the entire story of every single life. His ability to see every detail clearly is a definitive feature. He knows precisely what each person chooses to believe, and whether or not someone is going to accept Jesus Christ as Lord and Savior. Free will is not an issue that presents any impossibility to God, because God knows what everyone would have chosen under any circumstances at any time. He is in every minute with us at the same time. He sees the past, present, and future all at once. Time does not exist for the Lord as it does for us. He observes the 2D picture as well as the 3D experience. In the end, risking a simplified summary that will seem Molinist but appeals to the timelessness of God, *God knows what we chose.* God knows what we will choose,

---

7. A main proponent of Molinism is William Lane Craig, who has produced multiple helpful resources on the topic. Compare his short discussion "Molinism vs. Calvinism"; and see Compelling Truth, "Theological Concept of Middle Knowledge."

because God has already been on the other side of our choice. He is in that moment of our choice, the moment of the distant future, and the moment at which we were born—all at once. Time is a measurement for us. It is not a limitation for God, but rather a limitation of our ability even to grasp the concepts of God's omniscience and omnipresence.

C. A Temporary Universe

Even as we live through time, we are asked to live as if we focus on what is outside of time. The Bible is clear that our world is temporary and that the heavenly realm presents a deeper, stronger, and eternal reality. Second Corinthians 4 puts it this way:

> 16 *But though our outward man perish, yet the inward man is renewed day by day.* 17 *For our light affliction, which is but for a moment, worketh for us a far more exceeding and eternal weight of glory;* 18 *While we look not at the things which are seen, but at the things which are not seen: for the things which are seen are temporal; but the things which are not seen are eternal. (2 Cor 4:16b–18)*

Verses like 2 Corinthians 4:16–18 emphasize the true nature of time. Time is real here, and it does matter. However, it is only limited to the holographic image of the universe, which is passing away. Second Corinthians 4 underscores the sharp distinction between our temporary, three-dimensional world, where we do not see what is coming next, and the eternal world, which views our universe as a projection that is going to disappear. Ironically, what we see is temporary; what we do not see is eternal.

What this verse implies is that the physical world is a form of illusion that is passing away. This world is only a semblance of reality. Just the same, the relatively lesser reality of our universe does not mean that God is misleading us about the nature of our existence. On the contrary! He tells us what is being done with this world, even though we may not be able to understand it (see Amos 3:7; Isa 55:8–9; and John 15:15). It is when we have the misapprehension that ours is the highest or the only reality that we deceive ourselves.

Holographic images, whether they are assumed to be simulations or not, share an important definitive feature: whatever else they may be, they are images, not originals. Like two-dimensional photographs, holographic images capture pictures of reality. They embody aspects of an original object.

The Bible and the Holographic Universe

Kostas Skenderis explains the holographic universe model in these terms:

> About 100 years ago, quantum mechanics and general relativity changed the way we view physical reality. The idea that the universe is a hologram is similarly a paradigm-shifting idea. It suggests that there is a deeper structure in space and time.[8]

Skenderis is not making a statement about God or reality as defined by the Bible, but is rather seeking to communicate how the holographic principle works or might affect scientific theories in the future. His last phrase here is striking: "*It suggests that there is a deeper structure in space and time.*" Our reality is not as "deep" as everything goes. Something bigger and better defines it and shapes it. We might think of it this way: a holographic universe is defined by something bigger and more profound than itself. "Whatever we see around is a holographic projection of a bigger reality."[9]

The rise of holography as a medium for film, art, and scientific analysis raises cultural issues that emphasize the temporary and challenging nature of holographic images. What do holograms indicate about the nature of reality and illusion? In a 1990s discussion, Eduardo Kac explores questions of context, illusion, and representation as they relate to reality. A large element of his study relates to how understanding holographic images changes or expresses people's perceptions of the world around them, especially in regards to time and temporality. Kac notes the transience of holographic images as he explains that viewers of the image comprehend the existence of something that is being shown in the image. In other words, viewers of the image know that they are dealing with an object that does not share the same level of reality as the object captured in the image. A holographic image is an expression of stored information. "The person who tries to grab the [holographic image of an apple] knows that he/she is not looking at an apple."[10] By reaching out for the holographic apple, that same person is not seeking to be deceived into thinking that this is a real, original apple, but is instead appreciating the sharp contrast between the image and the real.

Another illustration of the distinction between a holographic image and an underlying reality occurred in 2012, when American rapper Tupac Shakur performed at the Coachella Valley Music & Arts Festival in

---

8. Waugh, "We Will Find Out."
9. Batiz and Chauhan, "Holographic Principle," 675.
10. Kac, "Photonic Webs," section "3. A Hologram Is Not a Picture."

Time and Knowledge

California. Appearing side by side with fellow rappers Andre Young ("Dr. Dre") and Snoop Dogg, Shakur roared a greeting to the eighty thousand people in the crowd and performed two songs for the audience. However, the performer was not the real Shakur, but a facsimile of him. This Shakur was a holographic image. In reality, Tupac Shakur had died over fifteen years before. Although the holographic Shakur addressed Coachella as Coachella, the real Shakur passed away before the Coachella Valley Music & Arts Festival even began.

Despite the fact that the holographic Shakur was lauded for its realism, the unrealism of the Coachella Shakur was primary. Everyone who knew of Shakur would know that the rapper was not actually present to perform onstage. The creation of the holographic image had nothing to do with the reality of Shakur's death prior to the performance, because as real as the image might have been, the existence of a holographic copy could not bring Shakur back to life. People expected the holographic image to be part of a temporary and momentary experience. Coachella Shakur looked real. "He" moved, acted, and apparently interacted. Yet "he" was only a short-lived projection evoking memories of the original. No matter the half-million-dollar price tag for the Coachella creation, or how believable the image might have been to those at the festival; Coachella Shakur was still only ever an ephemeral entity, forged by holography.[11] Unreal Shakur's existence made an impact on fans, but it did not cancel out the real Shakur's existence, and it could not affect the reality of Shakur's death almost two decades earlier.

While virtual tours and posthumous appearances have become increasingly popular in the wake of the Coachella hologram, the relative unreality of holographic images draws attention to the comparison between what is real and unreal.[12] Those who experience such holograms recognize that the images are those of late celebrities or, in other cases, of performers who are not performing in person. Their temporary nature does not of itself notably diminish audiences' appreciation. The appearance of deceased singers or speakers has not caused cultural collapse due to the impermanence of the holograms. By and large, people recognize that the holograms are temporary opportunities to relive the past or to imagine a

---

11. Kaufman, "Exclusive."

12. Tomorrow's World Today, "Becoming 3D"; and Dodson, "Strange Legacy." Further details of the hologram's creation and general reactions to the event can be found in Ganz, "How That Tupac Hologram"; and Perez, "Holograms."

different present or future. At any rate, notably, the audiences' responses and reviewers' opinions do not have any effect on the reality of the holographic images. The holograms may have an influence, but they do not gain any material substance merely because they are influential and realistic.

The distinction between the permanent and impermanent, the real and unreal, extends to a much broader level of significance for daily life. When we define our universe as a holographic image, by implication, we gain a better understanding of what the Bible means about "a far more exceeding and eternal weight of glory." Our 3D view of momentary experience is limited. We live in the moment, not unlike the holographic rapper who was bound to the world of the stage and brought to existence for a short period of time. By contrast, as the (more) real audience conceived of space and time very differently from how the Coachella image would have had it been sentient, and as the audience had life beyond the festival's grounds and could leave the area, God sees what we will be and where we are going. His experience is far fuller than the Coachella audiences' could ever be, and is not bounded by any limited perception of space and time. He sees the 2D, 3D, and every other dimension of our existence. He sees what Skenderis calls the "deeper structure."

The "deeper structure" of spacetime is something that God tells us about through His Word. Creation itself points to the "deeper structure," as well, causing many people to be more open to the temporary nature of our universe. Scientists who do not believe in the Bible are examining the universe and concluding that a 2D external view of it exists. They are coming to believe that this universe is a projection or a simulation of some kind. As they are recognizing, the universe is passing away in some form. Where it is going and where it came from, they disagree—and they are still searching for answers. Thankfully, however, the Bible gives us the answers to the puzzle of our universe's past, present, and future.

D. Our Limited Understanding

In accordance with the holographic principle, the universe is more immediate to those who are part of the simulation. Like characters in a book, we don't see what comes next. To us, the simulation comes complete with a past, present, and future. It is a place of suspense and, much of the time, uncertainty. We do not comprehend how times and events fit together or what they mean. One of the quintessential Bible passages illustrating our

Time and Knowledge

limited understanding from within the holographic universe is found in the "love chapter" of 1 Corinthians 13:

> 9 *For we know in part, and we prophesy in part.* 10 *But when that which is perfect is come, then that which is in part shall be done away.* 11 *When I was a child, I spake as a child, I understood as a child, I thought as a child: but when I became a man, I put away childish things.* 12 *For now we see through a glass, darkly; but then face to face: now I know in part; but then shall I know even as also I am known.* (1 Cor 13:9–12)

In verse 12, the word "darkly" is a translation of the Greek phrase ἐν αἰνίγματι (*en ainigmati*).[13] Αἰνίγματι/*ainigmati* is a form of αἴνιγμα (*ainigma*), the source of the English word "enigma." An "enigma" in Greek is a "riddle." The phrase ἐν αἰνίγματι/*en ainigmati* essentially means "in a riddling way," or "in a riddle," and therefore "darkly," "obscurely," or "dimly."

Passing through a worldly existence in a physical body, we have a limited perspective from our earthly position. We cannot see clearly. Without the Holy Spirit, we cannot see at all (see Matt 13:11). However, for Christians, it is a joy to seek out clearer vision; it represents the treasure of knowing God more closely.

When we catch glimpses of the spiritual, or find traces of it around us, we are seeing the barest outline of a shadow of the reality that is mostly invisible to us. If nothing else, spiritual warfare is evidence of an outside, unseen reality. Ephesians 6:12 explains, "For we wrestle not against flesh and blood, but against principalities, against powers, against the rulers of the darkness of this world, against spiritual wickedness in high places." We do not see everything that is real.

Second Kings 6 gives another famous glimpse into the invisible reality of the supernatural world. In this passage, the Syrian king is desperate to capture the prophet Elisha. Learning that Elisha is in Dothan, the king sends troops against the city. What comes next is fascinating:

> 15 *And when the servant of the man of God was risen early, and gone forth, behold, an host compassed the city both with horses and chariots. And his servant said unto him, Alas, my master! how shall we do?* 16 *And he answered, Fear not: for they that be with us are more than they that be with them.* 17 *And Elisha prayed, and said, Lord, I pray thee, open his eyes, that he may see. And the Lord opened the*

---

13. Cf. LSJ, s.v. "αἴνιγμα."

eyes of the young man; and he saw: and, behold, the mountain was full of horses and chariots of fire round about Elisha. (2 Kgs 6:15–17)

The dramatic revelation of the spiritual forces surrounding Elisha and his servant is suggestive of our own veiled vision. Often, the supernatural realm is physically hidden from us, as it was from Elisha's servant. How can we live with awareness of the spiritual world which we cannot see? We exercise faith knowing that the spiritual domain does exist, and that it is more real and eternal than anything we are familiar with on this earth. As 2 Corinthians 5:7 puts it, "For we walk by faith, not by sight."

The entire Bible testifies to the fact that God gives us pictures of a reality outside of what we think we know. The more intently we study the glimpses and God's direct interactions with humans as a group or as individuals, the more we can learn about the future the Lord has planned for those who are willing.

8

Truth and Substance

31 *Then said Jesus to those Jews which believed on him,
If ye continue in my word, then are ye my disciples indeed;*
32 *And ye shall know the truth, and the truth shall make you free. (John 8:31–32)*

A. About Absolute Truth

LET'S SAY THAT THE universe is holographic. If our world is an image or a simulation, is there any absolute reality? How do we know that anything is real? When Christians speak of God and moral laws, we say that God is the standard for right and wrong. He provides us with moral codes and teaches us the distinction between righteousness and sinfulness. Thus, we say that there is an absolute truth.

Conversely, proponents of relative truth argue that there is no such thing as an enduring right and wrong beyond what each individual person, or perhaps society, decides. "True for you but not for me" is an essential tenet of relativism. Even though that idea may sound fine in theory, it is unworkable. Relative truth is no more sustainable in daily life than in philosophy. Consider the logic of the argument. Someone who asserts that absolute truths do not exist is making an absolute statement: the person is *absolutely* claiming that absolute truths do not exist. In attempting to make

The Bible and the Holographic Universe

a relative statement and decry absolute truths, the relativist is acting as an absolutist—saying that truth is absolutely not absolute. And if the same person argues that the only absolute truth is that truth is relative, then another problem arises. What standard can be used to prove that there is only one absolute truth? Who decides the absolute truth that relative truth is the only absolute truth? Why and how? Logically, relative truth is insensible and unfeasible. "No worldview can be true if it contradicts itself," notes philosopher Paul Copan.[1]

Practically speaking, relative truth has other problems. Natural laws represent one of them. If truth is relative, why is gravity so absolute that we cannot walk off cliffs without falling? Why is there a reaction for every action? Why can we not walk through walls no matter how much we believe we can? Nature does not accommodate relative truth.

In the realm of personal ethics, other pragmatic dilemmas present themselves. If person X attacks person Y for no reason, does Y have the right to complain or fight back? On a personal level, would you be upset if someone suddenly attacked you, even if he said your discomfort might be true for you but not for him? Society based on relative truth is subject to rules made by those who are powerful. However subjective the rules themselves may be, they turn out to be the rules desired by people with the means or ability to enforce them. "Might makes right" is an inevitable guideline. (As a college student, in a discussion with a self-avowed agnostic who insisted that truth is relative, I met with a vivid illustration: the same agnostic who argued "might makes right" became angry later the same day when he received a poor grade in class, and declared that the professor had "no right" to give him a B instead of an A.)

But does the holographic universe undo all of these arguments? Does truth have to be relative because the world around us is a simulated reality?

Even though some scientists and philosophers say yes, they always come back to the same challenges of first cause and origins. What started the simulation? Can we have a hologram without a higher reality? Asserting that *no* universe is real involves forming assumptions based on relative truth, where nothing can be true except for relative truth. And again, that claim is an absolute statement. So what if the Bible is right? What if an absolute reality beyond our universe actually does exist, and explains why

---

1. Copan, *True For You*, 24. On various cultural manifestations of relativism, see Copan, *True For You*, 19–20.

our universe operates as it does? Then we would have an answer that makes sense of the objective universe which our world copies.

In other words, the holographic image leads us back to the validity, if not even the necessity, of absolute truth. This is not only true because the science of the holographic principle is based on an absolute assumption about the nature of entropy and black holes, but also because the holographic image appears to be a copy or shadow that operates on other absolute principles. One of these other principles is cause and effect. Another is the imminent end of the holographic image. The existence of a holographic universe might make the world appear to be relative because it emphasizes how unreal we may be—until it becomes clear that a higher reality is inevitable, and that it suits the biblical dynamic.

B. Temporary World, Permanent Reality

Regarding our universe as a holographic image should emphasize a) the fragility we have in the world we see and hear around us and b) the permanency of enduring absolute truths.

The entire Bible stresses how tenuous human life is. As solid and secure as this world might seem, our lives are only a wisp of vapor. James 4:14b reads, "For what is your life? It is even a vapour, that appeareth for a little time, and then vanisheth away." "So teach us to number our days," says the Psalmist, "That we may gain a heart of wisdom" (Ps 90:12).

Constant reminders of our fleshly nature's insufficiency underlie our need for Christ and redemption. Still, God has a plan that incorporates and manages our temporary, failing nature. He was aware of what would happen to the universe before setting it all in motion. He arranged a reconciliation with us for that reason, if we are willing to take advantage of the ultimate display of real love and compassion. If we accept Jesus Christ as Lord and Savior, the Atonement for our sins, then we have the promise of new life that outlives this holographic simulation. The key is not living for today or for ourselves.

First John says,

> **15** *Love not the world, neither the things that are in the world. If any man love the world, the love of the Father is not in him.* **16** *For all that is in the world, the lust of the flesh, and the lust of the eyes, and the pride of life, is not of the Father, but is of the world.* **17** *And the*

The Bible and the Holographic Universe

world passeth away, and the lust thereof: but he that doeth the will of God abideth for ever. (1 John 2:15–17)

The Greek word for "world" in these verses from 1 John 2 is κόσμος (*kosmos*), the English word "cosmos." A cosmos relates to a harmonious system or arrangement, and thus, to the world as a whole. Κόσμος/*kosmos*, defined as "order," or "arrangement," is related to the verb κοσμέω (*kosmeō*).[2] Among other things, κοσμέω/*kosmeō* means "to order," "to arrange," or "to set in array." Because ordering, arranging, and arraying are tightly knit with concepts of enhancing something and making it more attractive or fit for a purpose, κοσμέω/*kosmeō* also means "to adorn," or "to equip."

While the Greek κόσμος/*kosmos* refers to the world or universe as something that is set in order and arranged, closer examination of the word's origin highlights the transience of the world we know. The world—the κόσμος/*kosmos*, our cosmos—had a beginning and was set in a particular order by God. This order and arrangement is temporary. As John says, it is passing away. The order is going to be undone; its equipment is going to slip away.

Much further back than the ancient Greek, the proposed etymology for κόσμος/*kosmos* is a word root in what is called "Proto-Indo-European." (Proto-Indo-European, or PIE, is the hypothetical mother language from which modern Indo-European languages are derived, and reconstructed from linguistic studies of ancient texts and modern languages.) The suggested verbal root for κόσμος is *$\hat{k}$oNs-mo-/*$\hat{k}$eNs-, which refers to putting something into an order or arrangement "by speaking"—that is, by declaring.[3] With this root in mind, we may have a better appreciation for the cosmos, the world, as something that was spoken into existence and order by God in Genesis 1.[4] The cosmos is something that was declared, not accidentally formed. God speaks the universe into existence in Genesis 1. Even more precisely, God declares and orders the specific details of the holographic universe, as recorded in the account of Genesis. Indeed, the things of this world are all passing away. This would include the holographic elements that belong to the holographic world. Someday, the holographic world will come to its end.

---

2. Cf. LSJ, s.v. "κοσμέω."
3. Beekes, "κόσμος"; and Lubotsky, "Indo-European Suffix *-ens-," 156–57.
4. "And God said": Gen 1:3, 6, 9, 11, 14, 20, 22, 24, 26, 28, and 29.

C. Problems of Materialism

Unfortunately, since we live as "characters" in the holographic universe, we are easily convinced that "today" represents the true, lasting reality. We often think that our reality is the only world that endures or has any value. What we physically see limits our spiritual vision.

Focusing on the world around us rather than on the spiritual things we do not see is a form of what is called "materialism." This kind of secular materialism emphasizes the importance of material things in the physical world. It may represent an obsession with the material world. At the very least, it can reflect a mindset that concentrates on the material world and de-emphasizes immaterial things, such as intellectual and spiritual concerns.[5]

Philosophically speaking, the theory of materialism, also occasionally known as "physicalism," is a radical rejection of the non-material. In general, physicalists opine that all real items in our universe, including objects that are apparently non-physical, are physical in some sense. All elements of nature, including moral, social, and psychological aspects, are considered to be physical or to relate to the physical world in a consequential way.[6] Everything is seen as hinging on the physical, material world.

Materialism was one of many worldviews explored by King Solomon in the book of Ecclesiastes. When he set out to find meaning in life, Solomon investigated a broad range of philosophies and ideologies. Although he was conducting his search in the tenth century BC, his pursuits have great relevance for us today. Solomon was gifted with amazing wealth and resources (see 1 Kgs 3:13 and 2 Chr 9:22) and had the ability to gather any physical goods his heart desired. He built, acquired, and bought and sold. "And whatsoever mine eyes desired I kept not from them," he recalls (Eccl 2:10a). Yet Solomon's extreme materialism failed him. He realized that physicalism, like every other human philosophy and venture, is vanity (Eccl 12:8).

The Hebrew word for "vanity" in these passages literally refers to a breath or vapor. Figuratively, the word denotes something that has no substance or worth.[7] Even as he observes that material objects are worthless, Solomon is stating that they are transitory, like a breath of air. They have no

---

5. As demonstrated by the discussion in Merriam-Webster Online, "Materialism," definition 2.

6. Stoljar, "Physicalism," abstract.

7. Bible Hub, "1892. hebel" (*Brown-Driver-Briggs*).

The Bible and the Holographic Universe

eternal meaning in themselves because they are mere vapor. In this sense, everything material is fleeting and futile.[8] The description is fitting for a holographic world in which nothing material is anything other than encoded information.

Embracing materialism as a philosophical framework is not always as deliberate a choice as it was for Solomon in his experiment. "Many people unconsciously assume that matter is the only reality," writes mathematician and apologist John Lennox. "The truth is, matter is not even the primary reality. Jesus taught that God is spirit (John 4:24), so spirit is the primary reality. Matter is derivative: *All things were made through him* (John 1:3)."[9]

The treatment of matter as a secondary reality or state of reality cuts to the heart of the issue for modern thinkers who are troubled by the holographic principle. If the higher reality is, from our point of view, immaterial or non-physical, a dilemma quickly arises. What meaning does life have? If acquisition and material substance hold no real significance, what does? Solomon finally reached the solution that God alone holds the answer to that question. The Preacher admonishes his readers to focus on the Lord and what is pleasing to God, rather than to the self (Eccl 12). Solomon may not have been expounding on the holographic principle as a formal hypothesis or conducting mathematical models with black hole simulations, but he was addressing the relevant questions at the crux of human existence. If the universe is a fleeting image surrounded by a far larger, more realistic, and enduring reality, the materialism of today rapidly will become a nothing of yesterday. Without Christ, this summary of the human condition is overwhelming, or, at the very least, condemning.

As Christians surrounded by material items and belief systems, it is easy to become wrapped up in the idea that the material world is all that really exists. And the trend of concentrating on the material rather than on the spiritual frequently reveals itself in the ways that institutional churches have come to conceptualize their mission. Many pastors and churches fall into the trap of watering down the message of the Gospel in order to attract more attendees or to become more "culturally relevant." Others embrace the notion of social justice to such an extent that they convince themselves Jesus would be willing to accept any values or behaviors, as long as people are being cared for materially. In these cases, physical materialism and comfort take over, and true spiritual substance and meaning are cast aside.

---

8. Cf. Bible Hub, "1892. hebel" (*NAS Exhaustive Concordance*).
9. Lennox, *Against the Flow*, 321. Italics in original.

D. From Materialism to Supernatural(ism)

Materialism undoubtedly influences the establishment churches or "church visible"; i.e., the church as a social institution or physical congregational group, as opposed to the invisible church comprised of all believers in Jesus Christ as Savior. At the same time, church-affiliated or not, much of America claims to believe in the supernatural. A 2017 Pew Research Center Survey found that 90 percent of Americans "believe in some kind of higher power." Of the 90 percent, 56 percent say they believe in the God of the Bible, 23 percent believe "in some other higher power / spiritual force," and 9 percent do not believe in God, but do believe "in some higher power / spiritual force."[10]

Meanwhile, Wiccanism and Paganism are making tremendous gains in the United States. Studies by Trinity College indicated that Wiccanism increased from 8,000 adherents in 1990 to 340,000 in 2008. Paganism boasted around 340,000 members in 2008 as well. In 2014, the Pew Research Center found that approximately 1 to 1.5 million Americans identify as Wiccan or Pagan.[11] Witches in America are not quietly conducting meetings in the background, either. They are openly holding rituals and inviting unaffiliated individuals to participate in ritual practices. For example, in 2017, witches worldwide announced that they were going to curse newly-elected President Donald Trump and circulated instructions for others to join them in casting "binding spells" against him.[12]

Witchcraft, astrology, tarot card readings, and other occult practices have only increased since the COVID pandemic. An entire social media community on TikTok shares videos of ritual practices and seeks to find spiritual connection and empowerment, using names such as "WitchTok" and "SpiritualTikTok" to denote the growing movement.[13] In 2020, psychic businesses experienced an increased demand in their online services, and the market continues to thrive.[14] "Right before COVID, I think people were finding a real interest in the spiritual world," comments "Long Island Medium" Theresa Caputo in a March 2021 interview. "Astrology, stones, crystals. Now it's even more so. We look for things that we can hold onto

---

10. Fahmy, "Key Findings," 1.
11. Singh-Kurtz and Kopf, "US Witch Population."
12. Musumeci, "Witches."
13. Bohra and Willingham, "'WitchTok.'"
14. Macdonald, "What, If Anything."

that give us faith or hope."[15] Caputo's remarks are echoed in the fact that many members of "Gen Z," the children of millennials, are fascinated by spiritualism of all kinds.[16]

Belief in the supernatural world is hardly waning. It is thriving. If anything, it is shifting from a belief in the biblical God to almost every other kind of supernatural force, or to any other conceivable, supposed higher power.

How can Christians strive to both recognize the true supernatural reality and be in the world, but not of it, especially when there is always so much deceit and confusion regarding truth? Recognizing the true reality has to involve developing a sense of discernment. We rely fully on the wisdom of God, not of people or other powers. Even as we deal with outside influences of materialism, paganism, and other demonic forces, we have to make an effort to fight against our own sinful nature. The truth of God has to be the baseline for everything we do. Winning the battle requires developing and practicing wisdom in accordance with biblical teaching.

> *The fear of the Lord is the beginning of wisdom: and the knowledge of the holy is understanding. (Prov 9:10)*

> **9** *And this I pray, that your love may abound yet more and more in knowledge and in all judgment;* **10** *That ye may approve things that are excellent; that ye may be sincere and without offence till the day of Christ. (Phil 1:9–10)*

> **6** *As ye have therefore received Christ Jesus the Lord, so walk ye in him:* **7** *Rooted and built up in him, and stablished in the faith, as ye have been taught, abounding therein with thanksgiving.* **8** *Beware lest any man spoil you through philosophy and vain deceit, after the tradition of men, after the rudiments of the world, and not after Christ.* **9** *For in him dwelleth all the fulness of the Godhead bodily. (Col 2:6–9)*

In short, being in the world and not of it, and seeing truth as it is, come from belonging to Jesus. He provides the only proper focus and source of being. In accordance with that truth, Jesus compares us to sheep, needing a shepherd. He is the Good Shepherd. His own sheep know their Shepherd.

> **2** *But he that entereth in by the door is the shepherd of the sheep.* **3** *To him the porter openeth; and the sheep hear his voice: and he*

---

15. Crandell, "Long Island Medium."
16. See Greene, "Study"; and Jaradat, "Gen Z's Looking."

calleth his own sheep by name, and leadeth them out. **4** *And when he putteth forth his own sheep, he goeth before them, and the sheep follow him: for they know his voice.* **5** *And a stranger will they not follow, but will flee from him: for they know not the voice of strangers. (John 10:2–5)*

I am the good shepherd, and know my sheep, and am known of mine. (John 10:14)

My sheep hear my voice, and I know them, and they follow me. (John 10:27)

Recognizing real reality starts with recognizing the real identity of Jesus Christ.

9

Conforming to Reality

*. . . even God, who quickeneth the dead,
and calleth those things which be not as though they were. (Rom 4:17b)*

A. Information Decay

ONE OF THE QUALITIES of informational "bits," like those that make up our imperfect universe, is that information is impermanent. Information naturally decays over time.[1] This decay occurs for a number of reasons. The information may become outdated or so efficiently accessed that it no longer holds value.[2] Most importantly for our purposes, information can be lost from a system due to corruption.[3]

Data corruption entered our universe at the fall in Genesis 3. Since that time, the information that comprises the holographic image has been decaying and losing integrity. The bits and pieces that comprise our universe are corrupt.

We know from the Bible that our universe has an end. The universe must be replaced by a new heaven and new earth, which are not and will

---

1. Rajaram, Rupanagunta, and Kumbakonem, "Data Assets," 30.

2. Rajaram, Rupanagunta, and Kumbakonem, "Data Assets," section "Why Does Information Decay?"

3. Smith, "Cost."

not be corrupted. From the moment when humanity embraced sin and obtained a sinful nature, our world has been marked for destruction. Why? Because it came under the bondage of sin and imperfection. The sinful, fleshly nature, tied to the holographic image, is irredeemable:

> *For he that soweth to his flesh shall of the flesh reap corruption; but he that soweth to the Spirit shall of the Spirit reap life everlasting. (Gal 6:8)*

The promise through Christ is that we as individuals can be redeemed into a state that is incorruptible.

> *Now this I say, brethren, that flesh and blood cannot inherit the kingdom of God; neither doth corruption inherit incorruption. (1 Cor 15:50)*

> *3 According as his divine power hath given unto us all things that pertain unto life and godliness, through the knowledge of him that hath called us to glory and virtue: 4 Whereby are given unto us exceeding great and precious promises: that by these ye might be partakers of the divine nature, having escaped the corruption that is in the world through lust. (2 Pet 1:3–4)*

Christians eagerly wait for the physical realization of the redemption we have been promised through Christ. Furthermore, creation is waiting with us.

> *19 For the earnest expectation of the creature waiteth for the manifestation of the sons of God. 20 For the creature was made subject to vanity, not willingly, but by reason of him who hath subjected the same in hope, 21 Because the creature itself also shall be delivered from the bondage of corruption into the glorious liberty of the children of God. 22 For we know that the whole creation groaneth and travaileth in pain together until now. 23 And not only they, but ourselves also, which have the firstfruits of the Spirit, even we ourselves groan within ourselves, waiting for the adoption, to wit, the redemption of our body. (Rom 8:19–23)*

The end of the holographic image is the end of the corruption. Data loss and information decay are terminated when the system itself is terminated. With the conclusion of the image, we will receive the full manifestation of the promised newness and freedom. Creation itself will be made new. Now, waiting for the end of this simulation, all of this creation groans under the weight of its slavery. Here, the nature of a holographic image that is losing information and that is corrupted only highlights the point that there has to be a reckoning of the current image and a revelation of reality. The old universe, the broken and fallen creation, literally cannot go on forever.

B. In the Image, but Not of It

In the midst of a corrupted simulation that is aching to be undone and replaced, how can we be in the holographic world but not of it? After all, our bodies are part of the holographic image, and are equally impermanent. Jesus spoke of our predicament in these terms in the prayer recorded in John 17:

> *14 I have given them thy word; and the world hath hated them, because they are not of the world, even as I am not of the world. 15 I pray not that thou shouldest take them out of the world, but that thou shouldest keep them from the evil. 16 They are not of the world, even as I am not of the world. (John 17:14–16)*

Even though we cannot elect to leave the world and physically separate ourselves from it, Christians are no longer "of" the world. According to John 15:19, we have been "chosen . . . out of the world." Our conformation to the ways of God separates us from the secular world because we are being transformed from the inside out.

Paul instructs us to set ourselves apart from the world by such inner transformation in Romans 12. In seeking to know and serve God, we are severed from the thought patterns of the world:

> *And be not conformed to this world: but be ye transformed by the renewing of your mind, that ye may prove what is that good, and acceptable, and perfect, will of God. (Rom 12:2)*

Paul does not mean that it is necessary for us to approve God's will in order for it to be good, acceptable, and perfect. If that were needed, then God's standards of good and evil, which are external to the holographic image, would not represent absolute good and evil. They would be subject to the internal whims of the image. If that were the case, the ways of God would be in *and* of the image. As it is, truth is external to our world, but defines the workings of our world. Truth is in the image, but it is not of the image, because it is not defined by the image. The goodness, acceptability, and perfection of God are not determined by human experience or desire.

Conforming to Reality

Christians cease thinking the way that the world thinks when we internalize the Word of God and live out our faith. We leave behind our sinful habits, behaviors, and views. God's will and the standards imparted in the Bible do not change to fit us so that we can become Christians. The Bible is a mirror for us as we will be. In it, we see what we are becoming.

> 23 *For if any be a hearer of the word, and not a doer, he is like unto a man beholding his natural face in a glass:* 24 *For he beholdeth himself, and goeth his way, and straightway forgetteth what manner of man he was.* 25 *But whoso looketh into the perfect law of liberty, and continueth therein, he being not a forgetful hearer, but a doer of the work, this man shall be blessed in his deed. (Jas 1:23–25)*

Scripture is a static, unchanging place for the reflection of God's glory. Because we are conforming to true holiness, God's glory is the glory that is showcased in our transformation. We are intended to reflect the same values and honor for God that we find in the Bible. Such godly virtues and reverence are abhorrent to us in our sinful nature; our lens of morality is completely misaligned, connected to a limited-time and limited-perspective hologram under a curse of willful rebellion against God. Coming to Jesus entails recognizing sin as something that is evil and requires repentance. The whole relationship is built on the inherent distinction between Jesus and us. Our relationship with the Bible is therefore also altered when we become Christians, because the biblical worldview becomes our own. The Bible is a mirror for the liberty we have in Jesus. It is a mirror for us as we are transformed into godly people of the Word.

Our relationship with Jesus fundamentally changes what we are. If we are like characters in a giant holographic story, it would be ridiculous to suppose that a holographic character could give itself real life and escape from the hologram it was created to inhabit. The character is part of the larger program. From the inside, it lives through the story. However, if the hologram's creator intervenes and makes the character more than a hologram, or adjusts its programming so that it is not dependent on its holographic habitation, then the character can become something more. This is precisely the amazing change that happens to us when the Holy Spirit enters into us, as we accept Jesus Christ as Savior. We become truly alive, for we have "passed from death unto life" (John 5:24b; see also 1 John 3:14).

The description from the holographic principle is still a poor one. God does so much in making us alive in Christ! It is impossible for us to truly comprehend the depths of God's goodness, or to understand the full implications of our redemption through Jesus Christ. Our efforts to be *in* the world but not *of* it must be centered on prayer and reading of Scripture.

C. Prayer and Seeking God

Prayer is vital to our relationship with God. First, it represents our communication with the Lord. We speak to God in prayer. Praying is an opportunity to:

- express praise and thanksgiving (1 Tim 2:1 and Col 4:2);
- repent (2 Chr 7:14 and Prov 28:9);
- make requests for ourselves and others (Mark 11:24; Phil 4:6; and Jas 5:16);
- receive strength and revelation (Jer 33:3; Matt 26:41; and Luke 21:36).

Paul summarizes these qualities of prayer in Philippians 4, proclaiming, "In every thing by prayer and supplication with thanksgiving let your requests be made known unto God" (Phil 4:6b). Supplication is an act of request and appeal, indicating an expectation that the one who receives the request is in a superior position. Thus, supplication comes with an awareness of submission on some level. We need something from God. Supplication is to be paired with thanksgiving. God has answered prayers in the past, and ought to be thanked for doing so. He should likewise be thanked for being faithful and compassionate in the present. Every day we receive mercies of God. The ability to pray and personally come before God through Jesus Christ is an amazing privilege worthy of our thanks. No wonder Paul reminds the Philippians to be grateful and express adoration in their prayers!

Paul adds that prayer has results. "And the peace of God, which passeth all understanding, shall keep your hearts and minds through Christ Jesus," he says (Phil 4:7). Prayer should be constant and meaningful, and it is far more than a ritual practice. Notice that Paul does not promise that each individual will immediately or automatically receive the desired response from God. God answers, yes, but no matter what the answer to the specific prayer request or praise may be, we have an absolute assurance that surpasses every need. We are given the peace of God. This is a peace that "passeth all understanding." It is not limited to the moment or to the duration of the universe. The peace of God is past our comprehension. Through

Conforming to Reality

Jesus, it lasts into eternity, giving us an enduring guarantee of our relationship with God.

This description of prayer leads us to another critical point: prayer in faith acts out our expectation that God hears us and is interested in engaging with us. He listens, and wants us to know it. Otherwise, what is the point in speaking at all?

Relationship is a two-way street, though. Even though the modern church as a whole does not often consider repentance to be as vital as grace, God "heareth the prayer of the righteous" (Prov 15:29). Grace is critical to our relationship with God, but grace is granted by God. It is a free gift (Rom 5). Still, grace is only one side of the relationship. Every human being has the choice to refuse the gift of grace. The second part of the relationship is a responsibility on the part of each individual. We must cry out to God with humble hearts. God's grace is demonstrated in that we are heard. Psalm 66 says,

> **18** *If I regard iniquity in my heart, the Lord will not hear me:* **19** *But verily God hath heard me; he hath attended to the voice of my prayer. (Ps 66:18–19)*

God is always listening to the repentant heart. His grace is intended to draw us closer and closer, even though we so often misunderstand it. The heart that is truly seeking tastes the Lord's goodness and wants more. God's grace and goodness are not about giving us the license to sin, but instead freedom from the eternal condemnation resulting from sin.

> **1** *What shall we say then? Shall we continue in sin, that grace may abound?* **2** *God forbid. How shall we, that are dead to sin, live any longer therein? (Rom 6:1–2)*

The more time we spend in prayer and the Word, the more we are transformed. The process of speaking with God changes us. His answers also change us. The recorded prayers of Jesus are an excellent example. While Jesus as God in the flesh was not changed as a result of praying, the prayers offered by Jesus exhibit these important points. Jesus always seeks for God's will to be done, and always yearns for the glory of God to be revealed (Matt 6:9–10; John 17:1, 4–5). His prayers are a demonstration of God's heart. "And I have declared unto them thy name, and will declare it: that the love wherewith thou hast loved me may be in them, and I in them," Christ says (John 17:26). Real wisdom, real love, and real relationship are among the results of spending time with God in prayer.

The Bible and the Holographic Universe

In general, prayer is an action that leads us closer to understanding our proper role in creation, or in the holographic image and beyond. Our relationship with Christ is a bridge between the holographic universe and reality.

> 11 For I know the thoughts that I think toward you, saith the Lord, thoughts of peace, and not of evil, to give you an expected end. 12 Then shall ye call upon me, and ye shall go and pray unto me, and I will hearken unto you. 13 And ye shall seek me, and find me, when ye shall search for me with all your heart. (Jer 29:11–13)

God is revealed to us in the face of Jesus Christ as well as through prayer and the Bible. How we respond is up to us as individuals. Our response determines our eternal destination.

D. Improving the Program?

One of the current obsessions of the establishment church in western nations is making the world ready for the return of Jesus. The church institution has come to think and teach that we should be focusing on social justice, a world order of peace and safety, and a border-free union providing for the needs of everyone. Often, in this view, the church plays a pivotal cultural and societal role in reshaping the world to make it as close to perfect as possible. A result of this idea is that it causes proponents to downplay the importance of Israel in God's plans. They may become convinced that the church has replaced Israel as God's chosen people. Known as "replacement theology," this belief is not always associated with a theology of making the world better for Jesus' return. Even so, it is not uncommon for modern churches to teach that the church's job is to improve the world so that Jesus will come back.

The modern church as a whole has increasingly rejected the literal interpretation of end times prophecy. By denying that Revelation (for example) is a prophetic book, much of the church implicitly believes that everything can get better and better. Some therefore think that the church's role is to serve as God's chosen ones and to help prepare the world for an ideal system, or at least for a coming golden age when all people are saved and have everything they could need or want.

How does this relate to the holographic universe? Despite having ambitious goals, characters inside a holographic program cannot successfully change the program or its limitations. They cannot fully grasp the bigger

Conforming to Reality

picture of what they are facing. Neither can we. Our best intentions are based on limited understanding. What's more, we have the Bible telling us very specifically that we are not to concentrate on fixing the world. Instead, our objective is to win as many souls as possible for Christ. The world is broken, but God is not looking for help in adjusting or repairing it.

Many Christians and church denominations are manifestly more concerned with fixing the world than telling it about Jesus Christ, the only One who can fix it. One illustration is responding to current events with stated goals for an improved and shared future, expressing a desire to reshape systems and "co-create" an altogether different type of world.[4] Despite some of the finest intentions of sincere believers, the idea that Christians have a mandate to work with the world and co-creatively transform political structures is mistaken. Though we are certainly called to love and care for others, our calling is not to pursue social change over spiritual rebirth. True spiritual need is the most severe problem plaguing the world. The church as an institution was created by God to preach the Gospel and to display God's glory, not to create a more ideal world at the cost of spiritual truth (see Matt 5:16; Eph 3:8–12; and Eph 4:17–24).

While we should exercise compassion, seek goodness, and love mercy in accordance with God's definitions of these values (see Mic 6:8), we should not expect either that any cooperative effort with the world will result in a more improved, better evolved, or more compassionate world system, or that the world is going to share or accept the biblical framework for what improvement and compassion can even look like. Rather than concentrating on a goal of building a better world, we are to understand that the world will hate Jesus, and will therefore hate us (Matt 10:10–39; Luke 21:34–36; Mark 8:36–37; and John 15, e.g.). We are not called to create a different physical world that operates in accordance with God's will; such a world will never come about through any semblance of earthly unity. We are to share the good news that every human soul has the opportunity to choose eternal life in Christ and to be prepared for the world that is following closely on the heels of our material reality (see John 6:9, 35–40, and 63).

Another example of misunderstanding of the church institution's role is the type of statement or public prayer that pleads with God to bring together all of humanity as children of one Father.[5] The Bible is clear that we become children of God by making individual decisions to accept Jesus as

---

4. For an example, see Parsons, "PC(USA) Stated Clerk."
5. See the approach of Episcopal Relief & Development, "Prayer for Peace."

The Bible and the Holographic Universe

Lord and Savior (John 1:12 and 3:18; Rom 8:14–16). Yet the ideas of "co-creation" and an ecumenical gathering of the people of the earth go far back in history to the Tower of Babel in Genesis 11. Not all unities have appropriate end goals, as far as the biblical worldview is concerned. It should be noted that in the rebirth of a global order under religious auspices, numerous Protestant denominations are walking in step with other religious systems that pray for the ability to "co-create" a regenerated world of complete fellowship. This reimagining does not particularly or necessarily associate that new world with the coming of Christ.[6]

Still, no matter who the person or party is, the problem is the ideological drive behind these kinds of prayers, political statements, and other declarations. Although such prayers may be united in their direction, the fact remains that they are looking in the wrong direction. All of humanity's attempts to restore the fallen world are in vain. We do not have the wherewithal to rebuild creation. We cannot restore anything in our own image, and certainly we cannot do it in God's image. We cannot "make it all okay."

God understands our deficiencies. He never asks us to try to repair the broken world or instructs us to pray for strength to fix the world. The Bible explains that healing comes only after and through the ultimate return of Jesus Christ, and not before. John witnesses the fulfillment of the promised newness, as we read in Revelation:

> ¹ *And I saw a new heaven and a new earth: for the first heaven and the first earth were passed away; and there was no more sea.* ² *And I John saw the holy city, new Jerusalem, coming down from God out of heaven, prepared as a bride adorned for her husband.* ³ *And I heard a great voice out of heaven saying, Behold, the tabernacle of God is with men, and he will dwell with them, and they shall be his people, and God himself shall be with them, and be their God.* ⁴ *And God shall wipe away all tears from their eyes; and there shall be no more death, neither sorrow, nor crying, neither shall there be any more pain: for the former things are passed away.* ⁵ *And he that sat upon the throne said, Behold, I make all things new. And he said unto me, Write: for these words are true and faithful.* (Rev 21:1–5)

Notice that our heaven and earth do not become the eternal reality. The holographic image will never replace what is fully real. God does not enter

---

6. Cf. Catholic Online, "Prayer for World Peace, 1978" (see section "Peace Prayers"); Boudreaux, "World Religious Leaders"; Winfield, "Masked Pope, Faith Leaders"; United Nations, "World Religious Leaders"; and other examples at Oikoumene World Council of Churches (see section "Church and Ecumenical Relations" under "What We Do").

Conforming to Reality

into the hologram to take up permanent residence. He pulls us out of the hologram, as we see in the Bible. The rest of Revelation 21 and 22 detail the glory and beauty of the new creation (see Rev 19–22).

Second Peter 3 expounds on the promise that this world is not destined for restoration. Healing is for the souls saved out of the simulation, but not for the elements of the simulation that exist (2 Pet 3:10–13). Peter says that "the heavens shall pass away with a great noise, and the elements shall melt with fervent heat, the earth also and the works that are therein shall be burned up" (2 Pet 3:10). "Nevertheless we," Peter adds, "according to his promise, look for new heavens and a new earth, wherein dwelleth righteousness" (2 Pet 3:13).

Peter tells us that through God's promises, through the knowledge of Jesus, we become "partakers of the divine nature, having escaped the corruption that is in the world through lust" (2 Pet 1:4b). Our world is indeed utterly corrupt. Jude 23 instructs us to hate "even the garment spotted by the flesh."

The entire Bible is about the insufficiency of flesh. Simply put, the world lies under a curse. The simulation is corrupted. We cannot and should not try to fix it. Should we love, seek justice, act in humility and mercy? Absolutely. But those qualities are not defined by humans, any more than the church is defined in relation to social activism or governmental influence. The church is meant to serve Jesus Christ first. We are not here to ready the world for Jesus' return and try to make the simulation a good enough place for the establishment of God's physical kingdom. We work to share the Gospel so that souls are ready for Christ's return and will be prepared to leave the simulation when the time comes.

Hebrews 12 instructs us to keep our eyes on Jesus. When we're busy working on making the holographic world a "better place," we're distracted from our real mission of telling others that there is a real and better place beyond the hologram, and that it is waiting for those who accept Jesus Christ.

10

Origins and Spiritual Illusions

25 *Of old hast thou laid the foundation of the earth:*
and the heavens are the work of thy hands.
26 *They shall perish, but thou shalt endure:*
yea, all of them shall wax old like a garment;
as a vesture shalt thou change them, and they shall be changed:
27 *But thou art the same, and thy years shall have no end. (Ps 102:25–27)*

A. *The Matrix*, Universal Illusions, and Spirituality

THE IMPLICATIONS OF A virtual universe or simulated universe are intertwined with those of the holographic universe. If the universe is a holographic projection or a computer simulation, we who live inside it are only as material as the rest of the projection or simulation. However, the most crucial part of us—our spiritual nature—still cannot be explained away. The same problem about the origins of the illusion of the universe applies to our lives. "Where did the universe have its beginning?" becomes a question of "Where does the spark of human life come from in the first place?"

Because *The Matrix* represents for many people the quintessential example of simulated universe in action, the franchise has underscored the ramifications of a world that is an illusion or relatively lower form of

Origins and Spiritual Illusions

transient reality. At the time of the second and third *Matrix* movies' releases in 2003, the spiritualism of the *Matrix* series was especially widely discussed. An article by NPR author Rick Karr illustrates the type of conversation that was taking place. Karr first considers the work of Jake Horsley, a filmmaker writing on the (meta)philosophy of the Matrix. Horsley has argued that we live in the dream world of a distracted civilization. He contends that our life-experiences are far more comprehensible in light of the theory that reality is a dreamworld, and that there are indeed unseen entities controlling our world.[1] To contextualize Horsley's interpretation of the Matrix, Karr cites Frances Flannery-Dailey (Associate Professor of Religion, Hendrix College). Flannery-Dailey states that Horsley's views reflect early Gnosticism. Gnosticism holds that this world's creator was some sort of a lesser god, and not a supreme deity. It further treats Christ as an emissary of knowledge imparted to humanity from another reality, and considers our world as evil by virtue of its materialism.[2] Flannery-Dailey notes that *The Matrix* combines elements of Gnosticism and Buddhism: the two, she said, "pose humanity's fundamental problem and solution in the same terms—ignorance and enlightenment."[3]

The complicated web of worldviews in *The Matrix* and its successors has not been lost on Christian reviewers. "From a Christian perspective, *The Matrix* is a mixed bag," *Christian Answers* contributor Jason Murphy summarily reports.[4] Brian Godawa (Christian Research Institute) identifies multiple Gnostic elements of *The Matrix*. Human beings in the series are not slaves to sin; instead, they are unaware of who they truly are. They desperately need to be awakened to the nature of reality. For the humans in the Matrix, salvation is found in realization of their actual situation, and not in freedom from sin.[5]

There is a prevailing notion of spirituality that is frequently connected with *The Matrix* and similar concepts of the world. Such spirituality is typically a form of mysticism. Regardless, it is critical that we recognize that religions like Buddhism, Gnosticism, and others are not tied to the

---

1. Compare the discussion of Horsley's book and *The Matrix* by Karr, "Spiritual Message."
2. For more on Gnosticism and gnostic cults, see Martin, *Kingdom*; and Got Questions Ministries, "Christian Gnosticism."
3. Karr, "Spiritual Message."
4. Sic. Murphy, "Matrix."
5. Godawa, "Matrix."

The Bible and the Holographic Universe

holographic principle itself. The validity of the holographic principle *per se* has nothing to do with these systems.

Let's be clear: from a biblical perspective, even if our world is holographic, these false religions' claims are *still not true*. Buddhism, Gnosticism, and other belief systems are not necessary to make sense of a holographic universe or a simulated world. Again, these systems are not any more accurate under the circumstances of the holographic universe than they are without the holographic principle. A holographic universe would not automatically make false belief systems true simply because proponents might agree that a physical universe is not the highest reality. For one thing, if anyone says that these systems must be true because they assert that our world is not the ultimate reality and the holographic universe is not the ultimate reality, then the same person should logically be proving the truth of Christianity, which actively affirms that ours is not the highest reality. The result would be a paradoxical problem. You cannot believe that other belief systems and Christianity are both accurate; they are mutually exclusive. Either the God of the Bible is the one true God as the Bible says, or not. The holographic principle does not provide any credibility to unbiblical world systems. Just because other faiths claim the world is not permanent does not mean that they should be regarded as more credible than the Bible. The Bible explains that the universe is not permanent, but in the context of a very distinct worldview.

In the same vein, the holographic principle does not in itself "prove" that the Bible is true. Our primary evidence comes from other sources: archaeology, historical accuracy, and internal consistency, for example. Considering that prophecy alone has repeatedly been trustworthy in interpreting world events and predicting events to come, the Bible has far more to offer than other belief systems. Does the holographic principle fit with the biblical worldview? Yes. Is the Bible disproven if the holographic principle is demonstrated to be untrue? No. This specific explanation for the nature of the universe is not requisite for believing in the Bible and in Jesus Christ. A holographic universe does not threaten Christianity. Just the same, Christians should be aware that the Bible can make sense of the holographic universe as well as of the universe's beginning, present status, and end.

The idea that underlies the Matrix and similar notions of virtual worlds is a form of the "simulation hypothesis," formally set forth by philosopher

Origins and Spiritual Illusions

Nick Bostrom.[6] The simulation hypothesis is related to the theory of the holographic universe because both are based on the concept that our universe is all based on information rather than physical matter. The simulation hypothesis is only one way of explaining what the holographic universe would be or how it came into existence. Bostrom's argument is that universes that are computer simulations are more likely to exist than non-simulated universes. Statistically, Bostrom proposes that simulated beings are more likely than biological beings. Summarily, his hypothesis rests on the assumption that a civilization with the capacity to create such impressive simulations would not be limited in its ability to create millions upon millions of other simulated civilizations. The crux of the matter is the amount of power necessary to create or direct the simulations.[7]

The Matrix features a virtual world designed by sentient Machines who enslaved humanity for energy. The Machines' sentience is an underlying cause of the downfall of human civilization. Human sentience itself is now restricted to the simulation called the Matrix. That is, the Matrix is all that most humans ever really know. The simulation hypothesis plays out in the existence and worldview of the vast majority of humans in the story. Bostrom's philosophical take does not explain the world of the Matrix, though. Human sentience led to the development of mechanical sentience, which has in turn subjugated humanity. Whether or not the original human condition was one of virtual simulation is a non-issue in the original series. Humans who have escaped the Matrix have no idea of life before the Machines. While *The Matrix* shows a form of the simulation hypothesis and a virtual world in action, and its universe is an illusion, the movies still do not have much information about the real world beyond the Matrix in the premise of the trilogy. And for those who apply the Matrix to our reality, the same strictures would apply: How could we have knowledge of any "higher reality" as a certain source of knowledge? Without the Bible, this is a very real question.

The Matrix illustrates the point quite well. Our view of reality outside of the Matrix is restricted throughout the first three movies in the *Matrix* franchise. A very few humans either live outside of the computer simulation or are rescued from it and brought into the real world. There, humans live in an underground city called, interestingly enough, "Zion." The trilogy left room for sequels and entire storyworlds that could ask the question of

---

6. Illing, "Are We Living."
7. Illing, "Are We Living." Cf. Greene, *Hidden Reality*, 274–306.

The Bible and the Holographic Universe

whether or not Zion actually is part of a larger Matrix, and just as virtual as the recognized Matrix simulation. This space for imagination offers viewers the opportunity to wonder over and over about the truth of the Matrix and its boundaries. For this reason alone, the trilogy's presentation of the Matrix evoked and continues to evoke cultural memes, at the same time provoking thoughts about the definitions and construction of "reality" and "unreality." Several generations of moviegoers, familiar with several generations of different types of technology, have now had *The Matrix* as a springboard for asking questions about where virtual reality or unreality meets actual reality. At its heart, however, the Matrix embodies the pressing concept that our universe is an illusion composed of non-physical bits of information. If our world is a simulation like the Matrix, it's nothing but computer code and abstract programming.

Bostrom's philosophical approach to an illusory universe relies on an understanding of the universe as pure information, as asserted by the holographic universe idea. Importantly, information theory does not necessarily require the universe to be a computer simulation. But more recent developments in our understanding of how information works would seem to suggest that our universe is an illusion—and studying the nature of information helped lead physicists to what we today call the holographic principle, a theory that leads us back to the bigger questions of spirituality and what we call "reality."

B. Exploring the Origins of the Holographic Image

The conclusion that we live in an image implies that the image is a picture of something or that it is a projection. If this is the case, it suggests that the image is a result of a process or the copy of an original. Theoretically, according to this principle, something more permanent exists beyond the image. And so the holographic principle raises a big question about origins. Where did the holographic image come from? If the image is a simulation, like a running computer program, then the question is just as pressing—even perhaps more so.

Even if the image in question appears self-sufficient, something sparks it into existence. Our universe is actually so advanced and detailed that it supports the need for a Creator. Such is the entire argument for Intelligent Design, the view that "the design of living systems—and even the nonliving

Origins and Spiritual Illusions

elements of the universe—suggest a Designer."[8] Somewhere, in the deeper structure, there is a more objective vantage point. Who or what sees the universe from this other vantage point, one that is higher than our own? For Christians, the answer should be obvious. God sees from the most objective view possible. The more we know the Lord and appreciate the world as described in the Bible, the closer we come to understanding the true nature of reality as well as the universe in which we live.

Not everyone agrees that the holographic image would prove the existence of someone or something outside of our universe. Many researchers are working to develop a multitude of theories to explain away the need for and objective reality of God as the Creator of a universal illusion.[9] They do not want science to lead them in the direction of evidence for a divine Creator, or at least not for the God of the Bible.

It has always been difficult to remove God from inside the holographic image. No matter how loudly or fervently human beings try to drown out its voice, creation does indeed cry out with the need for a Creator (see Rom 1:20). Removing the Lord from the reality beyond the simulation proves just as difficult, if not more so, than dismissing God from the simulation. Even physical laws which can be observed in practice here within the image are theoretical outside of the image because we do not directly observe them there.

What we can do is extend the method of reasoning that has been used across the ages. We can make logical inferences based on observed physical laws. Since we see chains of cause and effect here, we have good reason to assume that cause and effect holds outside of the image, too. Here, a simulation is started and created by something; it makes sense to assume that the same would also be true there. The same factors that point to God's existence here presumably point to it there as well.

In our universe, it would go against logic and observed scientific laws to say that a simulated reality is the highest reality in a system. Simulation or not, the holographic image cannot be the highest reality unless it violates the cosmological argument. The cosmological argument is a style of argumentation that addresses, among other things, the need for a first cause. "The durability of the argument and the stature of its defenders is eloquent testimony to the fact that to man this world is somehow just not sufficient of itself, but points to a greater reality beyond itself," William Lane Craig

---

8. Answers in Genesis, "Intelligent Design."
9. See also Miller, "Law of Causality."

affirms.[10] Logically, the argument for a first cause is the argument that nothing cannot come from nothing. There is no logical place for an infinite regression leading to nowhere.

Atheism in particular has to consider how everything came into being if God does not exist to be the first cause. By definition, God is an uncaused cause. He is the cause of everything else. Again, for atheism, which rejects God, the origin of the universe presents a problem. If the universe is holographic, how could it not require someone or something to generate it or to turn it on in the first place? This conclusion about first causes is irksome to many who want a way to deny God.

The Bible has a solution. According to Genesis, God spoke everything into an ordered, logical existence. Rather than claiming that everything came from nothing, the Bible states that everything was designed by God. God had no beginning and will have no end. His eternal existence explains the universe's temporary existence. Starting from God alone and caused by God alone, the holographic image can make sense.

C. Panconsciousness and Panspermia: Self-Generation, Extraterrestrials, and More

What about a universe that could have caused itself, or an illusion that jump-starts its own existence? As recently as 2020, a team at Quantum Gravity Research in Los Angeles has proposed that a simulated universe actualizes itself ("self-actualizes"). This group suggests a concept called "timeless emergentism." If the holographic principle indicates that our reality is actually a construct, these researchers assert, then the nature of our universe may align with long-held ideas of certain Eastern philosophies. This would mean that the universe we know is a "mental construct," rather than a material one. Spacetime is a result of that reality's own efforts to comprehend the construct. According to this argument, the mental construct subconsciously forms a whole host of beings and objects. In turn, they provide opportunities for relationships and the investigation of all possible outcomes.[11]

---

10. Craig, *Cosmological Argument*, xi, providing an overview of the argument's history and typology. For shorter and less comprehensive treatments, see Reichenbach, "Cosmological Argument"; Slick, "Cosmological Argument"; Ligonier Ministries, "First and Primary Cause"; and Hodge, "Cosmological Argument."

11. Ratner, "New Hypothesis."

Origins and Spiritual Illusions

The simulation hypothesis is not precisely the same as the holographic principle, but it is a type of argument for the universe as an illusion. Researcher James B. Glattfelder describes the simulation hypothesis as "the most popular version of a simulated universe." Not only is our three-dimensional reality an illusion, as the holographic principle elucidates, but (as conveyed by the simulation hypothesis) the source of the illusion is a larger reality (i.e., ontological framework) that surrounds or contains it.[12]

The same Quantum Gravity Research team that promotes a self-actualizing universe connects its model to the concept of a panconsciouness or panpsychism. In the realm of self-actualization, everything is about what you think and imagine. Just as dreams are small, private, and primitive "simulations," so too (allegedly) is everything in the universe the product of self-generation. Notably, we observe nothing like this self-generation in actual practice. Even though people have dreams, dreams are illusory. They are not material substances, and they do not have a physical effect on our reality. Having a dream does not make the dream become a reality.

Imagination works in a similar way. We can imagine almost anything, and when we do, we can bring our imaginative worlds to life by creating stories, films, or three-dimensional models. Book series and movie franchises offer escapes into whole other worlds. Be that as it may, these worlds are not self-generated. We initiate them or contrive them based on others' imaginary premises. These worlds are not proven to have any substance in themselves.

In other words, the idea that the universe generates itself through a joint consciousness or through people's general thoughts and beliefs has never been demonstrated to be feasible. In practice, passive self-generation does not happen. Active agency on some level is crucial to creation and imagination. Panconsciousness may seem to solve that problem by suggesting that inhabitants of a universe actively participate in imagining that world. Yet the apparent solution is no better than the problem; it simply pushes the problem back one more step. Compare the situation with artificial intelligence. The singularity hypothesis asserts that artificial intelligence (AI) will someday be able to upgrade itself and become more intelligent than the humans who created it. What happens next depends on the view of the person who is describing the singularity and the nature of

---

12. Glattfelder, "Universe Built of Information." For a variety of views, compare Kurzweil, "Questions and Answers"; Schulze-Makuch, "Reaching the Singularity"; Hvistendahl, "Can We Stop AI"; and Dhooper, "AI Trajectory."

The Bible and the Holographic Universe

artificial intelligence.[13] Whatever ensues, and whether or not AI is "safe" or "friendly," one basic point remains: the artificial intelligence had an origin outside of itself. Even if AI were to overtake humans today and build a "Matrix" to subjugate humanity, the artificial intelligence would have been created. It would have had a cause, since another source of conscious intelligence initiated it.

The allegations that our universe is a "mental construct" and that it generates its own spacetime both illustrate a very familiar human impulse. When human beings indulge in our sinful nature, we desire to push God out of the equation of our reality. The issue of locating a first cause for the universe has therefore been around since the beginning of time. Proponents for a non-God solution have been around almost as long. Many have been willing to accept virtually every alternative to God. When no alternative is available, they embrace theories that could (to their way of thinking) potentially move the need for God back a step. This should be a familiar situation to many Christians. We may have done much the same before turning to Christ. This does not mean that every scientific theory or hypothesis espoused by an atheist or agnostic is invalid or that we should be angry at researchers in these areas. The holographic principle, multiverse theory, and other concepts may very well be accurate, and the Bible already explains human nature for us. However, the scientific studies in question do not invalidate God, nor does the fact that advocates may use them as a way to try to avoid God.

But inevitably we come to another question about origins and a frequent approach of researchers. If God is not acceptable, why is a pan-consciousness or a supposedly self-generating something or someone else acceptable? According to the Bible, the reason is again humanity's desire to escape the necessity for God. Almost any suggestion that can remove God or reduce an immediate divine influence seems acceptable to those who do not want to reconcile with God or the implications of a divine existence. A similar proposed solution for the invention of the universe is the notion that life was transplanted to Earth from elsewhere. This is another hypothesis that could become caught up in the holographic universe theory before long. Here, certain advocates of evolution entertain the idea that life somehow arrived from somewhere else (a proposal easily found under the names "panspermia" or "exogenesis," with the transportation itself attributed to accidental processes or not) or that extraterrestrials "seeded"

13. Orlic, "Origins."

Origins and Spiritual Illusions

the earth (called "guided" or "directed" panspermia). In 1908, the Swedish chemist Svante Arrhenius imagined that panspermia was a process of "living spores wafting across the universe propelled by beams of starlight"; in 1981, atheist Francis Crick most famously described directed panspermia in his book *Life Itself: Its Origin and Nature*, where he considered that life on Earth may be the result of advanced extraterrestrials who came to our system using rocket ships and seeded the planet.[14] "That a Nobel Prize-winning scientist of Crick's standing would embrace what might be called a desperation theory of life's origins only reflected what he saw as the seriousness of the obstacles that stood in the way of accounting for the rise of life by more conventional means."[15]

Many of the people who advance these types of hypotheses are searching for a God-less solution to life. No matter how problematic a claim may be, proponents are seeking to find a non-supernatural starting point for sentient life and evolutionary processes so that they may dismiss the biblical God altogether.[16] Panspermia represents a necessary alteration to Darwinian evolution and its failure to explain the presence of Earth's complexities.[17] Rather than proposing that life on Earth began solely from materials available on Earth, despite all odds and observed natural laws, panspermia suggests that the seeds for life do not have to be located on Earth.

In 1985, Alan Hayward noted that anti-creationists would have to either adjust or reject their traditional views of Darwinian evolution in order to hold to any evolutionary theory. Hayward discusses the dilemma of evolutionary biologists who are seeking to "modify" Darwinism or to identify "an entirely new theory . . . to explain evolution." "So far they have not managed to find [such a theory]," Hayward says, "but they are still looking."[18] Panspermia and other evolution-friendly alternative approaches to life's origins can represent the type of theory being described by Hayward.

As much as proponents urge these ideas as alternative quasi-solutions to the pitfalls of Darwinian evolution, Christians should be extremely

---

14. Regis, *What Is Life?*, 98. Bates, "*Designed*," offers a concise Christian analysis of Crick's work and worldview. See also Europlanet Media Centre, "Could Life"; and Kaufman, "Did Life."

15. Regis, *What Is Life?*, 98.

16. See Frank, "What If Life"; and Klinghoffer, "Another Problem."

17. The failures of Darwinian evolution are set forth by Behe, *Darwin Devolves*; Morris, *Scientific Creationism*; Lubenow, *Bones of Contention*; and Cuozzo, *Buried Alive*, among others.

18. Hayward, *Creation and Evolution*, 21.

The Bible and the Holographic Universe

cautious in dealing with these concepts. We do know that demonic influences could easily make use of these hypotheses in order to gain a cultural foothold. Demons with supernatural abilities would not find it difficult to present themselves as humanity's designers and saviors.[19] It is for good reason that Paul warns the Corinthian believers to beware of "another Jesus," "another spirit," or "another gospel" (see 2 Cor 11:4). Also, Christians should be aware that panspermia, panconsciousness, self-generation, and other cosmological and philosophical views are not new and do not supersede the truth of the Bible.

Interpreting the holographic principle so as to try to explain away God raises as many questions as it appears to answer. Panspermia and similar hypotheses are likewise troublesome, especially if they become tied to the holographic universe idea. Their "solution" only poses the same old problem of origins, albeit one step removed.[20] Where did life come from if it was brought to Earth by someone from somewhere else? What caused life to exist, wherever or whomever it came from in the first place? This is nothing more than "kicking the can": shifting the responsibility back one step. That one step still goes back to something else that cannot be explained—that is, without the existence of God to create the universe and initiate life within creation.

That being said, guided or not, panspermia could offer supporters of the holographic principle an explanation for the universe. If extraterrestrials could have transplanted the seeds of life to Earth, might they not also have been the designers of a holographically simulated universe? Or would their existence hint at an entire chain of universes, one simulating or stimulating another *ad infinitum*? Once more, these questions do not have helpful answers, insofar as the universe's first cause is concerned. Either extraterrestrials (under these terms) are subject to the holographic universe's boundaries, or they are not. If they are not, then are we presuming the extraterrestrials or one main extraterrestrial is divine, and is the "god" for our universe? To say that an alien sparked the simulation into action leads us back to the issue of who the alien is. The Bible proffers itself as evidence of Who and what sort of Being God is. A panspermic alien hypothesis that rejects the Bible bears

---

19. Demonic deception in extraterrestrial affairs is a growing concern in evangelical Christian circles. Primary resources include Missler and Eastman, *Alien Encounters*; and Horn and Putnam, *Exo Vaticana*.

20. As discussed further by Behe, *Darwin's Black Box*, 248–53.

an additional burden of proof: it would be based on nothing but faith, unless that being, too, has made testable claims about itself.

Panconsciousness and panspermia don't solve any problems. Even if they appeal to the holographic universe, they still must come to terms with a non-coincidental fact: things start somewhere. Life begins somewhere. Where did *human* life first begin? According to Genesis 2:7, with the breath of God: "And the Lord God formed man of the dust of the ground, and breathed into his nostrils the breath of life; and man became a living soul."

Like life, simulations and holographic images have a starting point. Assume that the holographic universe is not the highest reality, or that it is comparatively "non-real," although events that happen here do determine eternal outcomes. How can a non-reality that *mimics* reality be a primary reality? Logically, can a simulation simulate something if there is nothing to be simulated? (Those familiar with the ancient Greek philosopher Plato's theory of forms may recall that Plato raised comparable questions, even though Plato is not a father of Christianity.[21])

Furthermore, if they were eternal programs without a beginning or ending, holographic programs and simulations wouldn't have a course to run. We know, however, that this is not the case. The laws of thermodynamics, like the logical cosmological argument, do not support the notion that our universe could have no beginning or end. Something must have started the universe. If not, then how do we explain the fact that our universe and the elements of our world wear down over time? Take the principle of entropy, which dictates that the usable matter and energy in our universe are decreasing. Entropy is a process that results in less available energy.[22] It is a process that occurs within the closed system of our universe. On some level, believing in entropy would involve acknowledging that newly accessible energy is not being added. The universe is aging. It has a definitive end-point.

So if the universe is indeed winding down as the laws of thermodynamics indicate, what comes next? What lies outside? Without God, our attempts to find new answers to these questions have repeatedly led nowhere. We go right back to where we started, facing the same situation and the same massively overriding questions.

---

21. Doyle, "Plato and Christianity."
22. See Merriam-Webster Online, "Entropy."

D. The Beginning of the Hologram

Does the biblical description of creation conflict with the holographic principle? Actually, although the Bible does not expressly require that our universe is holographic, its account of the world's beginning easily accommodates the idea. Genesis 1 emphasizes that God existed before creation.

> ¹ *In the beginning God created the heaven and the earth.* ² *And the earth was without form, and void; and darkness was upon the face of the deep. And the Spirit of God moved upon the face of the waters.* (Gen 1:1–2)

God was already present before the beginning of time. He has no beginning and end.

> *Thus saith the Lord the King of Israel, and his redeemer the Lord of hosts; I am the first, and I am the last; and beside me there is no God.* (Isa 44:6)

Accordingly, in Revelation 22, Jesus is the "Alpha and Omega, the beginning and the end, the first and the last" (Rev 22:13). Alpha is the first letter of the Greek alphabet; omega is the last. Before and after all things, there is God.

> *Before the mountains were brought forth, or ever thou hadst formed the earth and the world, even from everlasting to everlasting, thou art God.* (Ps 90:2)

A resounding implication of God's eternal, unchanging existence is that reality always already exists. God the Designer always is. He was there to initiate the simulation. By the Word of God, "things which are seen were not made of things which do appear" (Heb 11:3).

> ¹⁶ *For by him were all things created, that are in heaven, and that are in earth, visible and invisible, whether they be thrones, or dominions, or principalities, or powers: all things were created by him, and for him:* ¹⁷ *And he is before all things, and by him all things consist.* (Col 1:16–17)

Second Peter 3:3–5 describes people's decision to separate God from the act of creation.

> ³ *Knowing this first, that there shall come in the last days scoffers, walking after their own lusts,* ⁴ *And saying, Where is the promise of his coming? for since the fathers fell asleep, all things continue as they*

> *were from the beginning of the creation.* ⁵ *For this they willingly are ignorant of, that by the word of God the heavens were of old, and the earth standing out of the water and in the water.* (2 Pet 3:3–5)

The scoffers of the last days are willful in their ignorance (v. 5). Making mockery of the universe's origins, they challenge the biblical assurance that Jesus will return at all. Their intentional slight of God comes out of an effort to pretend that the world either popped into existence on its own or that something else initiated everything.

The word for "consist" in Colossians 1 is συνέστηκεν (*sunestēken*), a form of the verb συνίστημι (*sunistēmi*): "to be put together," "to take shape," or "to exist."[23] The same verb is used for "standing out" in 2 Pet 3:3–5. Everything that we see around us takes shape as it has been commanded to do by the Word of God. In terms of informational bits that comprise the holographic universe, we can say that God has called into being the information itself and then arranged it in meaningful patterns. These bits of information are invisible to us. God generated them out of nothing.

By the same token, the holographic universe is formed of things that are invisible. It is a projection built on light waves. In itself, it has no solid substance beyond the informational bits which God "put together" when He created our universe. Everything we see inside the simulation was made from things invisible, just as the Bible says. God spoke the word that initiated the simulation we inhabit. His higher reality was unaffected, but our reality began.

---

23. Cf. LSJ, s.v. "συνίστημι."

Epilogue

Regarding the Multiverse

LATELY, SCIENCE FICTION FILMS and television shows have brought another aspect of scientific hypotheses into public view: the idea of a multiverse. In particular, the Marvel Cinematic Universe and DC Comics worlds are popularizing the multiverse. While the multiverse is not necessarily always connected to the holographic principle, it is spoken of in the same breath by some proponents. Just as importantly, the concept of a "multiverse" can appear confusing or threatening to Christians who are wondering what it might mean.

The multiverse is the term for "(an) entire ensemble of innumerable regions of disconnected spacetime."[1] More simply, a multiverse is "a multiplicity of universes."[2] How many universes? No one knows. String theory suggests there may be as many as 10 to the five hundredth power universes (i.e., 10^{500}), each with somewhat distinctive properties, while a quantum multiverse operating under Hugh Everett's many-worlds interpretation (MWI) would imply that a universe exists to represent every possible contingent of reality.[3] In either case, a multiverse would basically be a group of universes which have their own space and time. Their inhabitants would

---

1. Andrei Linde explains the origin of the word "multiverse" in Kuhn, "Confronting the Multiverse."
2. Siegfried, "Making Sense."
3. Cf. Hooper, "Are There Multiple Universes?"; Hooper, "Hugh Everett"; Kuhn, "Confronting the Multiverse"; and Vaidman, "Many-Worlds Interpretation." But see also Moskowitz, "String Theory"; and Zweerink, "Multiverse Musings."

The Bible and the Holographic Universe

likely be living their lives and knowing nothing more than we do regarding universes outside of their own.

The multiverse is an issue because it represents something that may not be subject to human tests. We can reach our local universe, but the multiverse, while not actually a new hypothesis or model, is something different. It is the stuff of science fiction, and yet it is on the verge of scientific feasibility. In the words of science writer Stephanie M. Bucklin, the multiverse concept "straddles a strange world between science fiction and a plausible hypothesis."[4] Scientists grapple with the speculative nature of a multiverse. Some believe that we should be able to test aspects of it. Others contend that the multiverse must remain a matter of pure speculation and argue that we will never be able to do anything but form hypotheses about it. Stephen Hawking's final study before his death demonstrated his concerns about a multiverse as well. He was never comfortable about the idea of a multiverse because of its limited testability.[5]

Hawking's last study helps to show how the holographic universe could be related to the multiverse. Hawking and fellow researcher Thomas Hertog explain how holography may account for the possibility that we might live in a comparatively finite multiverse. Hawking and Hertog used string theory to reverse the perceived expansion of our universe and to describe the so-called "eternal inflation" of the universe. They tried to look back into the past in order to model what an earlier universe (in their view) might have looked like. They concluded that there was "a boundary in our past" and that we might be faced with a relatively "smaller range of possible universes" than the traditional multiverse.[6]

The notion of a limited collection of coexisting possible universes was at least more palatable to Hawking. The idea made for a multiverse that was more controlled and predictable. This type of multiverse was also more acceptable because it might allow for physical laws to vary. If laws are different in every universe within a multiverse, then physical laws that point to God's existence and demonstrate a need for a Creator could be explained away, because the laws we have would merely be one set among many. As Hawking puts it, "the local laws of physics and chemistry can differ from

---

4. Bucklin, "Is the Multiverse."
5. University of Cambridge (Research), "Taming the Multiverse."
6. See University of Cambridge (Research), "Taming the Multiverse." The study is available as Hawking and Hertog, "A Smooth Exit." On Hawking's 2010 treatment of the multiverse, compare Moffat, "Taking the Multiverse."

Epilogue

one pocket universe to another."⁷ Each "pocket universe" could have its own laws. These universes' different laws would allegedly not have to require God. They are simply laws fit to each universe, and nothing more, nothing less.

As an example, take the situation of Earth and its unique characteristics. Everything about Earth makes it singularly suitable for human life. Earth features exactly what humans need to survive. From its exact atmospheric composition and electromagnetic properties to its distance from the sun, Earth is the one known place in the universe where humans can survive, much less thrive. The fact is that the entire galaxy looks like it has been designed in order to accommodate human life on Earth. This principle is problematic for anyone uncomfortable with the concept of "design." If there is a design, does there not have to be a Designer?

The multiverse has recently come to the fore as a favored means of explaining away design and its Designer at the same time. According to one interpretation, the existence of a multiverse would imply that Earth and our universe are not so special at all. After all, if an infinite set or high number of universes exist, the probability of life increases. If enough universes exist, then one of them should coincidentally possess the qualities so essential to human life on Earth. Earth's unique suitability for life is then no longer an issue. For some proponents of the multiverse, the hypothesis offers the only feasible non-God explanation for a universe like ours. They see the multiverse as a necessary step toward understanding Earth's ecosystem and human life itself.[8]

Nevertheless, the dichotomy between multiverse and Creator is not so clear-cut as all that. As observed by physicist Steven Weinberg, the concept of the multiverse does not "[destroy] the possibility of an intelligent, benevolent creator." Weinberg asserts that both the multiverse and Darwinian evolution reduce the need for a kind Designer—but they do not eliminate it.[9]

The multiverse is not a problem for or proof against God. A multiverse can exist without having consequences for God's existence. At the same time, for those who are faced with the challenge of explaining Earth's design without recourse to a Designer, the multiverse may indeed be a critical tenet of belief. How else to explain the fact that everything seems so well-planned and fit for life? A quote from cosmologist Bernard Carr

---

7. University of Cambridge (Research), "Taming the Multiverse."
8. Folger, "Science's Alternative." See Carr, *Universe or Multiverse?*
9. Folger, "Science's Alternative."

The Bible and the Holographic Universe

summarizes the issue: "If there is only one universe, you might have to have a fine-tuner. If you don't want God, you'd better have a multiverse."[10]

Hence, for certain physicists, a hypothetical multiverse in a holographic simulation or set of simulations is a way of avoiding the need for God as Creator. However, the multiverse solution is not as much of a solution as it might sound. It requires an intense faith in what is unseen and entirely invisible. When the Bible speaks of faith, conversely, it refers to trusting that God will fulfill present and future promises based on prophecy and other visible, verifiable evidence from the past and present (see Hebrews 11).

For a Christian response to the multiverse, we have to consider several factors. First is that the multiverse is pure speculation. Second is that the interpretation of the multiverse as an escape from belief in God depends entirely on chance and odds.

Essentially, physicists who turn to the multiverse downplay the importance of conditions for life on our world. If so many universes exist, then it is much more believable, by some accounts perhaps even necessary, to expect that one universe among them would have the qualities exhibited here, in our universe. A very serious error in this approach is that it relies on mere assumptions. We might speculate what universes might or might not do with physical laws, and how they may or may not display evidence of design. In the end, the problem remains: our universe is our only basis for any scientific study or actual analysis. Everything else is conjecture that cannot be tested or observed.[11]

A very important third factor in the multiverse concept has already been mentioned, but deserves more elaboration. Despite the dogmatic assertions of some physicists who would rather reject God, the idea of the multiverse *per se* is *not problematic for Christians*. For one thing, we have no reason to assume that other universes would necessarily have other physical laws. Other universes in the multiverse might display the same characteristics that our universe does, and therefore exhibit their own evidence for the Creator's existence. Additionally, if other universes do exist, then the intricacy of a multiverse itself could be a significant manifestation of

---

10. Folger, "Science's Alternative." See Thomas, "'Multiverse' Theory"; and Miller, "Anthropic Principle."

11. Ross presents a helpful comparison between many physicists' position and the "gambler's fallacy" (Ross, "Anthropic Principle").

Epilogue

creative design. Instead of pointing away from God, the multiverse might point back to God.

How would a multiverse highlight elaborate design? For an analogy, let's look to the world of entertainment. An intriguing approximation of a practical multiverse theory is captured in the imaginative, expansive, and extremely *designed* "film universe" of Marvel movies. In 2019, Marvel Studios finished the famous "Phase Three" of their superhero films. "Phase Three" refers to the third installment in a series of movies with interconnected themes and characters. Phase Three officially began in 2016 with the third movie featuring the character Captain America (*Captain America: Civil War*) and ended in 2019 with the third movie featuring Spider-Man (*Spider-Man: Far From Home*). Phase Three was the last wave in what is called the "Infinity Saga," which was initiated in 2008 with the first *Iron Man* film.

Marvel's Infinity Saga of intertwined movie plots, all building to a grand climax with the 2019 movie *Endgame*, incorporated twenty-three individual movies into a deliberate multiverse construct. Grossing close to three billion dollars during its run in theaters, *Avengers: Endgame* became the biggest movie ever to hit the box office.[12] It and *Spider-Man: Far From Home* revealed that the Marvel Cinematic Universe (MCU) was already weaving together a diverse array of universes into a sweeping "multiverse" groundwork for future projects.

While the MCU has tended toward a single stream of continuity in all of its films, the revelation of a multiverse theory has allowed the studio to explain away any discrepancies with older Marvel franchises and to embrace new directions in Phase Four. Marvel is not the first studio to recognize the value of a multiverse theory. DC, Marvel's main competitor and comic book producer, has had its eyes on multiverse theory for quite some time. Unlike the MCU, the DC Extended Universe (DCEU) has not had a history of shared directors and writers behind its many films. Characters are radically different from one film or comic book incarnation to the next. DC has seen the multiverse concept as a way to deal with all of the issues that would otherwise arise from so many manifestations of characters and plots, embracing an approach that is much more individual in its construction of universes and concurrent productions. DC's chief creative officer, Geoff Johns, has stated that the studio regards all of its concurrent TV and film universes as part of a "multiverse." He adds, "For us, creatively,

12. Variety, "'Avengers: Endgame.'"

The Bible and the Holographic Universe

it's about allowing everyone to make the best possible product, to tell the best story, to do the best world. Everyone has a vision."[13]

The DCEU thrives on the distinction of worlds in which its characters live. For example, two different actors play the superhero Flash at the same time in different venues. One is a television show; the other, the Justice League movie series. The separate versions of the Flash are not a problem for DC, because the DCEU is based on a multiverse. Each Flash lives in his own world, or his own universe. At a minimum, he has his origins in his own universe. Furthermore, in *The Flash* television show that launched in 2014, the multiverse is a regular feature. The characters know that they are only one universe among many, and they have frequent engagement with the other versions of "themselves" from other universes in the multiverse.[14]

The DCEU shows how a multiverse can function with numerous, ostensibly unrelated universes unfolding at once. But one of the reasons that the MCU's multiverse of the Infinity Saga is particularly interesting for us is its demonstration of a creator's overarching, unifying guidance in a setting now revealed to be a multiverse. In a universe spanning twenty-three movies and culminating in a two-part sequence, a single producer, Kevin Feige, was involved in every film. There is no more need to remove God from the multiverse scenario than to claim filmmakers behind the Marvel Cinematic Universe were not necessary. In addition, Stan Lee, the creator of many Marvel characters, had cameo appearances in every MCU movie until his death in 2018. His last cameo role aired posthumously in *Avengers: Endgame*.[15] Yet no one uses MCU multiverse theory to argue against the existence of Kevin Feige and Stan Lee.

Kevin Feige and others directly engaged in the making of these movies or in the massive Marvel franchise were absolutely necessary to the creation of the MCU. The movies' cohesive, sensible network would not have suddenly sprung into existence. Nor does an MCU multiverse mean that Kevin Feige and other minds behind the movies must cease to exist. If the movies are set in a multiverse, do requirements for filming, acting, and production automatically vanish? No. The wider framework for writing and producing the movies does not change. As with the DCEU, having a host of actors, timelines, and plots does not mean that the movies and television series are not being produced in roughly the same fashion.

13. Wieselman, "Man at the Center."
14. Schaefer, "Flash: DCEU Multiverse."
15. Marvel Cinematic Universe Wiki, "Stan Lee."

Epilogue

Students and architects of fictional multiverses understand how multiverse physics avoids problems posed by space, time, and individual characters' storylines. In our real world, the holographic multiverse appeals to some physicists because of these same types of advantages. Accepting a holographic multiverse could be a way to avoid dealing with physical laws that point to a Creator, or at least to the God of the Bible. For a similar comparison, alternative-world writers of multiverse fiction look to multiverses as a way to expand storylines while doing away with continuity issues. The benefits of a movie multiverse are many, and they reflect real-world implications of a holographic multiverse. "[A multiverse] allows Marvel Studios to] go full-on comic book, introducing live-action versions of the Ultimate Universe and other realities from the Marvel comics mythos," writes popular culture author Adam Barnhardt.[16] For an illustration of multiverse advantages, here are a few of the conveniences Marvel (or DC) finds in embracing cinematic multiverses.

Among other things, the studio can:

- have continuity across multiple streaming and movie platforms;
- feature characters and worlds spanning dimensions, time, and space;
- follow numerous to infinite versions of the same character, possibly putting different actors in the role of one character;
- make "every element of fiction (into) canon"[17] (i.e., every franchise and movie owned by the studio is potential fodder and backstory for future films).

These opportunities are extremely attractive to moviemakers. Suddenly, everything is fair game. Flop or success, every previous movie can be wrapped up into a sweeping multiverse construct. Each movie presents its own universe or holds its own place within the primary universe. For a movie studio backed by thousands of story avenues or plot suggestions, a multiverse is a brilliant marketing move. "The MCU's multiverse is infinite," comments writer Michael Walsh. "Vastly different parallel worlds, along with vastly different realms of existence, all exist. Anything and everything can happen with them."[18] *Loki* and *What If . . .?*, two of Marvel's

---

16. Barnhardt, "Introduction."
17. Eisenberg, "How Marvel's Multiverse." Cf. Marshall, "How Disney Could."
18. Walsh, "Everything You Need to Know about the MCU's Multiverse." "The inclusion of the multiverse has heralded every bizarre story twist imaginable," muses Disney

The Bible and the Holographic Universe

first Phase Four television series, depend entirely upon multiverse theory, and demonstrate the multiverse's power as a medium for storytelling. The multiverse in fiction is a tool for telling not just one story, but every story, and oftentimes merely by implication.

But what about a multiverse in real life? Here the possibilities are equally enticing. A multiverse can allow for a universe where every single scientific hypothesis or theory is correct, whether or not it is true of our universe. Physics now does not have to grapple with the question of God. Additionally, if our universe appears to exhibit an absolute truth, philosophers can appeal to ignorance. Absolute truth might be different from one universe to another. In our universe, relative truth is a logical fallacy, because it is an absolute statement to claim that all truth must be non-absolute. Relative truth cancels itself out. But what if it could be different in another universe somewhere else? What if rules for how our universe operates mean nothing? Beyond all of that, a multiverse could open possibilities for movement across dimensions. Maybe human beings can encounter alternative selves of ourselves in other universes and learn higher truth from them. Maybe they could tell us more about our origins. Maybe we would come to another more malleable understanding of spacetime and find that there is no need for a universe to have an origin in the first place. After all, there could be a universe for every iteration of events. Like with the MCU, one universe is just the beginning. The significance of these implications is staggering.

True, not every physicist cites the existence of a universe for every single possible outcome that could ever exist. Some visualizations of the multiverse are more like Hawking and Hertog's described multiverse, with relatively contained or fewer universes. Whatever the case, the multiverse represents alternative worlds and alternate outcomes that are being played out somewhere and *somewhen* else. The implications are not so different from those that the MCU and DCEU continue to discover and reveal to their viewers.

These sweeping implications of a real-life multiverse are concerning to some. Because the many-worlds interpretation of the multiverse indicates a universe for every single human choice—meaning that a universe exists to represent every choice every individual could or would ever make at any point—the resulting multitude of countless universes is overwhelming. The possibilities are astounding, and go well beyond human imagination. Is it immoral to hope to live in a better universe? What constitutes compassion

---

fan Jett Farrell-Vega (Farrell-Vega, "Could Disney's").

Epilogue

in a series of universes where parallel selves encounter other circumstances? These representative questions are only a few of those raised in many different contexts.[19] Thus Rowan Hooper (*New Scientist*) refers to the multiverse as "an endless succession of what-ifs," introducing the concept as a "quantum moral maze." Hooper illustratively shares anxiety for how such an interpretation of the multiverse affects personal decisions and outcomes: "If many worlds is correct . . . my actions shape the course not just of my life, but of the lives of my duplicates in other worlds."[20]

In spite of these inhibitions, the multiverse is an appealing escape route. Looking back to the MCU analogy of an enlarging multiverse, in fact, we can see why some people would like the idea. Provided they interpret the multiverse as a comparatively abstract place where unlawful universes can or must exist, it offers them a way to fold everything into the reality we see and experience. For the same reason, various viewers express concern regarding the extreme leeway that a multiverse grants to Marvel's storywriters: "The Multiverse is dangerous in the wrong hands. Infinite possibilities also mean unlimited free passes for Marvel . . . No explanation is necessary. After all, 'anything is possible' now."[21]

Moviemaking can take the opportunities of a multiverse and plug them into an incredibly expansive collection of movies, characters, and franchises. The same benefits can also be exploited scientifically, *by presumption*. The ideas about how a multiverse could have contradictory physical laws are purely speculative. And they are still problematic for those who want to dismiss our physical laws in this universe. We don't know that other universes would not be bound by the same physical laws. We don't know that God, the Designer, would not have designed each one just as intricately, or with other demonstrations of power. Our physical laws indicate that the same physical laws should likely be in force elsewhere, too. To use the multiverse to automatically limit God and God's abilities is to conceptualize an escape from the reality we can test and prove, and to harness possibilities for unprovable hypotheses.

This kind of treatment of the multiverse is dangerous philosophically as well as scientifically. It is demonstrated in the sort of view of the

---

19. A fuller discussion can be found in New Scientist, *Quantum World*.
20. Hooper, "Multiverse Me."
21. Bradley, "MCU Just Supported." "Opening the core MCU to behemoth events . . . could prove to be dangerous," worries fan Chris Compendio (Compendio, "Multiverse").

The Bible and the Holographic Universe

multiverse that is cited by Sam Kriss (*The Atlantic*). Kriss expounds on potential negative effects caused by belief in a multiverse, worrying about the adverse impact on human imagination, sciences, and ambition. Believing in the multiverse, he says, may excuse away wrong answers, failures, and anything else that causes discomfort or messiness. On some level, a multiverse (at least in a many-worlds interpretation, where every possible world exists) "excuses every injustice; it's all been made good somewhere else, in the static infinity of the possible."[22]

Certain people may find that they prefer the multiverse theory precisely because of this type of reasoning. A slight twist on the meaning of a multiverse, and it can be used to make excuses against any considerations of intelligent design and the Bible's explanation for our Creator. For instance: if our world is just right for life and we want to assume from the outset that the reason could *not* be creation by God, then the earth's situation must be due to something else. And if we assume that every universe must operate differently, then belief in the multiverse is interpreted as "proof" that God doesn't exist . . . or at least doesn't *have* to exist. The assumption of different physical laws in different universes has never been proven, and likely never could be; it remains a matter of assumption and personal belief. This is multiverse theory taken on extreme faith. And again, this is not belief relying on faith that can necessarily be examined and tested. Conversely, faith based on the Bible can be investigated through prophecy, archaeology, and other areas of study.

The healthy development of science has never been able to proceed under conditions in which its practitioners are more interested in supporting ideology than in testing ideas. Science involves hypothesizing, testing, proving, theorizing. The multiverse presents a quandary because it cannot be tested by any realized methods. Still, to people who desperately want it to be accurate, or who must have it be correct in order to bolster their personal views, the multiverse offers vast possibilities. Until someone can definitively prove that the multiverse is wrong, it seems likely that there will be many who accept the multiverse on sheer faith rather than under the auspices of controlled scientific study, even to the point of accepting the idea that physical laws *must* be different in other universes.[23]

In short, the multiverse theory is untestable. Since it can never be tested, it is a virtually inexhaustible opportunity to deny or refuse to entertain

22. Kriss, "Multiverse Idea."
23. Cf. Scholes, "Can Physicists."

Epilogue

any evidence for God. If we can never understand the multiverse and yet insist that it offers us reasons to disbelieve in God, then we can always excuse ourselves from believing in God. In a way, this type of thinking represents agnosticism on the highest level. Yes, we may never understand the multiverse, but we have no reason to believe that the physical laws that may point to the existence of a multiverse are any different from one universe to another. As the DCEU and especially the MCU demonstrate, the formulation and operation of multiverses do not negate a need for consistent physical laws. Nor would the existence of a multiverse automatically negate the need for someone to carry out the creation, production, and care of the multiverse in question. Using the multiverse as an excuse to avoid talking about God is still a faith-based choice.[24]

So what about the Christian response to the multiverse? Could a real-life multiverse exist, holographic or not? The Bible never says it could not. God would be just as much God somewhere and somewhen else as in this universe. We would not have to assume that every universe presents a fallen world of sin and needs a Savior as we do. The Bible does say that Jesus died "once for all," as Hebrews 10:10 states. If we assume that other universes exist and that they have fallen creatures, it might also be that God has only chosen to extend salvation to human beings in our one universe. Perhaps we are truly the weakest among those in the multiverse. Paul does say that God chooses the foolish and weak to confound the wise and the mighty (1 Cor 1:27). Could that principle apply to our ranking in a multiverse?

These are big questions. For the moment, we seem to be unable to answer them. From a biblical perspective, that is okay. The end result is the same: whether or not a multiverse exists, the multiverse is not a problem for Christianity. Moreover, if physical laws in our universe support a multiverse, then they do so from a consistent starting point. They remain absolute laws for executing mathematical and philosophical models. The burden of proof should logically be on those who assert that observable laws are different somewhere and somewhen else. If existing physical laws suggest the need for God everywhere and every time they can be tested, then we are on stronger ground to believe that these laws represent consistent multiverse principles.

So again, even though some may allege that every universe must have different physical laws so that they can try to erase God, that allegation is just as untestable as the multiverse. If our reality points to God,

---

24. Answers in Genesis, "Faith in the Multiverse."

The Bible and the Holographic Universe

overlooking those indications is gross negligence, to say the least. Relying on untestable multiverse qualities in order to deny God or intelligent design is far more close-minded than entertaining the existence of God based on what we can test.

Ultimately, Christians should reject the notion that a multiverse either inherently opposes God or presents an alternative to the very idea of God. The multiverse in itself is not the issue. As astronomer Deborah Haarsma notes, to dismiss the multiverse outright "is to dismiss a rigorous, mathematical structure that is driven by curiosity about the nature of matter and gravity and our universe."[25] We ought to be wary of viewing any scientific interpretation or theory as something that would ever take the place of God. Like everything else, the multiverse should point back to the glory of God as unchanging, absolute, wonderful, and good.[26] We do not have to be afraid to pursue new ideas and conduct scientific research; truth does not shrink from honest study and experimentation.

The same goes for the simplest understanding of the holographic principle. As Christians, we never have to fear science. We should pursue knowledge and be involved in scientific discovery. Our faith is grounded on knowledge, evidence, and testability. Do we understand everything about the universe? No, no more than we could claim to know anything about the multiverse and physical laws that universes might or might not have. In the end, what matters is the One who created all of it. He is the One who sees the universe for what it really is—holographic, one of many in a multiverse, or something else we have never imagined. Someday, by the Lord's grace, we shall see and understand our existence for what it is. Until then, we live for that future, understanding that our place in the holographic universe is exactly what it is supposed to be: part of God's plan, forever and always.

Known unto God are all his works from the beginning of the world.
(Acts 15:18)

---

25. Haarsma, "Universe or Multiverse." Consider Hutchings, "Rewatching 'Spider-Verse.'"

26. As also discussed by Haarsma, "Universe or Multiverse."

Appendix A

Where to Learn More about Christianity

WHAT MAKES CHRISTIANITY UNIQUE? Why should anyone believe in the Bible as God's Word, or even in God at all? Is there other evidence for the truth of Jesus Christ as Savior? For unbelievers who are asking questions like these, or for believers who want to strengthen their faith in Christ, below is a very short list of some of the many resources regarding Christianity and the support for a Biblical worldview:

Ankerberg, John, and John Weldon. *Ready with an Answer*. Eugene, OR: Harvest House, 1997.
Associates for Biblical Research. https://biblearchaeology.org.
Christian Apologetics and Research Ministry. https://carm.org.
Craig, William Lane. *Reasonable Faith*. Westchester, IL: Crossway, 1994.
Defending Inerrancy. https://defendinginerrancy.com.
Geisler, Norman L., and Frank Turek. *I Don't Have Enough Faith to Be an Atheist*. Wheaton, IL: Crossway, 2004.
Kitchen, Kenneth A. *On the Reliability of the Old Testament*. Grand Rapids: Eerdmans, 2003.
Lewis, C. S. *Mere Christianity*. New York: Harper Collins, 1952.
McDowell, Josh D., and Sean McDowell. *Evidence That Demands a Verdict: Life-Changing Truth for a Skeptical World*. Nashville: Thomas Nelson, 2017.
Muncaster, Ralph O. *Examine the Evidence: Exploring the Case for Christianity*. Eugene, OR: Harvest House, 2004.
Strobel, Lee. *The Case for Christ/Case for Faith Compilation*. Grand Rapids: Zondervan, 2006.
Wallace, J. Warner. *God's Crime Scene: A Cold-Case Detective Examines the Evidence for a Divinely Created Universe*. Colorado Springs: David C. Cook, 2015.

Appendix B

How To Be Saved

Where Are You Going to Go After You Die?

CAN YOU ANSWER THAT question with certainty?

While this book has been mainly written from a Christian to Christians, some readers may not believe in Jesus Christ as Savior. If you are uncertain why you should believe in the Bible and Jesus, Appendix A offers additional resources for the evidence that supports Christianity. Like the rest of this book, Appendix A is a challenge to any unbeliever who is willing to examine the truth of the Bible with an open mind. Although not every Christian will agree with every section of this book, especially in relation to details of doctrine, every true Christian is defined by a common element: a personal relationship with Jesus Christ as Lord and Savior. If you deny that Jesus ever existed, if you think that the Bible is merely a book of lies and deceit, or if you believe that Christianity has nothing to set it apart from other faith systems, then consider Appendix A to be a direct challenge to you. Ask the questions and try to prove what you believe about Jesus and the Bible.

But maybe you have been reading this book and you realize that you do not have assurance about your own future. You may feel burdened by past failures or have a strong sense of meaninglessness. Perhaps you simply know that you want the something more that Jesus is offering you. You want to be saved, or you want to know what it really means to be saved.

How To Be Saved

What can you do to know that you are investing in a secure future and that you can be confident about the reality beyond our own?

The Bible promises that we can have absolute certainty about what will happen to us after we pass away from this world. We can begin to prepare for eternity now. According to the Bible, every human being is bound for an eternal destination in either heaven or hell. Heaven is a place of everlasting joy, security, and blessings in the presence of God. Hell is a place of unending torment, pain, and suffering, completely removed from any relief (e.g., Luke 13:3; Rom 1:18; Matt 5:29-30; and Rev 20:13-15).

> *He that believeth on the Son hath everlasting life: and he that believeth not the Son shall not see life; but the wrath of God abideth on him. (John 3:36)*

God, being absolutely perfect and holy, cannot dwell with imperfection and unholiness. He cannot abide the presence of any evil. Unfortunately, human beings commit countless evil deeds every day, and are perpetually thinking wicked thoughts. "For all have sinned, and come short of the glory of God" (Rom 3:23). Our sin makes it impossible for us to be with God. Sin demands judgment and punishment. It causes the death of the sinner. Furthermore, because it is naturally connected to what is imperfect and dying, sin means that sinners are always condemned ("For the wages of sin is death," Rom 6:23a).

Thankfully, God is a merciful God. He loves us, and has made a way for us to be washed clean of the sin that dooms us ("But the gift of God is eternal life through Jesus Christ our Lord," Rom 6:23b; see also 2 Pet 3:9b). Jesus Christ, the Son of God, came as God in the flesh. Despite never having committed any sin, Jesus willingly died for our sins. He then rose from the dead on the third day. His resurrection demonstrated perfect power over sin and created the opportunity for us to accept that death as an atonement for our sin (Rom 5:8). We therefore have only two possibilities for reaching heaven: living perfect lives, which is impossible because of our sinful human nature, or accepting Jesus Christ's death as the perfect atonement for our sins. Thus, only those who believe in Jesus will be able to spend eternity in heaven. Those who reject Jesus will forever be apart from God and all goodness, mercy, and pleasure. Rejecting Christ leads to eternal death in hell and prevents us from abundant life in this world (cf. John 14:6).

> **16** *For God so loved the world, that he gave his only begotten Son, that whosoever believeth in him should not perish, but have*

Appendix B

> *everlasting life.* ¹⁷ *For God sent not his Son into the world to condemn the world; but that the world through him might be saved.* ¹⁸ *He that believeth on him is not condemned: but he that believeth not is condemned already, because he hath not believed in the name of the only begotten Son of God. (John 3:16–18)*

Salvation only comes through Jesus. It begins in the heart and is supposed to be reflected in the Christian's actions. It involves turning to Jesus and away from the sins of the past. When you become a Christian, you admit that you are a sinner in desperate need of God's mercy. You must repent of your sin, understanding that you have done and still do wrong things, and that you need to make a sincere effort to reject sin. Being saved does not mean reciting a prayer and then forgetting about it, or feeling free to go on doing what the Bible says is wrong. You cannot save yourself by performing good works, and you are not automatically saved by virtue of God's love. To be saved, you must trust in Jesus as the Christ—the Messiah.

> *Neither is there salvation in any other: for there is none other name under heaven given among men, whereby we must be saved. (Acts 4:12)*

How Can You Be Saved?

> *Believe on the Lord Jesus Christ, and thou shalt be saved. (Acts 16:31b)*

1. Acknowledge that you are a sinner and that you have sinned. None of us deserve God's mercy, and we certainly do not deserve salvation. It is a free gift extended to us by Jesus, just because of love. You cannot earn it; you cannot buy it (e.g., Eph 2:8–9; Gal 2:16, 3:10–12; 2 Tim 1:9; Jas 2:10–11; Rom 3:20; and Isa 64:6). If you are oppressed by the weight of your sin, fear dying, are frightened by your own inadequacy, or know that there is nothing good in you, know that you can have pardon and relief through the sacrifice of Jesus Christ on your behalf (Titus 3:4–7).

2. Confess your sins before God. Admit that you know your sin condemns you, and that you cannot save yourself. The Bible says that the wages of sin is death. You cannot make up for the sins you have done, and you cannot save yourself. Realize that only Jesus can save

you from the sins you have done. Your sin is pulling you down to hell. It is keeping you from the reality that is worth living (John 6:47 and 10:9–10).

3. Call upon Jesus Christ as Lord, and believe that Jesus' crucifixion and resurrection mean you can be forgiven. Ask Jesus to forgive you of your sins and come into your heart as your Lord and Savior (Rom 5:9 and 10:13). Trust and have faith that Jesus has both the power and intention to save all those who repent of their sins, ask for forgiveness, and believe in the loving, merciful Savior.

> *That if thou shalt confess with thy mouth the Lord Jesus, and shalt believe in thine heart that God hath raised him from the dead, thou shalt be saved. (Rom 10:9)*

If you followed these steps, congratulations on beginning a new life in Jesus Christ. Christians are not perfect; we do not have to be perfect. But we are forgiven. If you admit that you are a sinner, repent, and believe in Jesus, confessing your sins to God and asking for salvation through Jesus Christ, you have a brand-new future (Gal 1:3–5 and John 4:14). As a Christian, you have the promise that you will go to heaven when you die. You now have a personal relationship with the God of the universe; you are a beloved child of God (1 John 2:25).

> *For the scripture saith, Whosoever believeth on him shall not be ashamed. (Rom 10:11)*

What Now?

Learn more about Jesus and your new identity as a Christian by reading the Bible. The book of John in the New Testament is a very good start for beginning your new life. Remember that your sins are washed away in the eyes of God. Seek to grow closer to Jesus by studying the Bible, praying, and finding a community of Christians who will support you. Maintain a repentant heart: do your best to turn away from your sins of the past by making decisions that are in line with the instructions of the Bible. Rest in the confidence of God's love and mercy toward you. Build your faith by spending time in the Word and focusing on an amazing, better future ahead. Your new life is just beginning, and the best, truest reality is yet to be revealed.

Bibliography

Alvarez, José Antonio Pozas. "What Is the Nature of Information?" *BBVA OpenMind* May 7, 2018. https://www.bbvaopenmind.com/en/humanities/beliefs/what-is-the-nature-of-information/.

Ambler, Marc. "Biblical Creation—Truly, a Theory of Everything (ToE)." *Creation Ministries International* May 14, 2013. https://creation.com/theory-of-everything.

Andrews, Travis M. "What If Life Were a Video Game? These 650,000 People Imagine It That Way." *Washington Post* December 22, 2020. https://www.washingtonpost.com/technology/2020/12/22/reddit-outside-video-game/.

Ankerberg, John, and John Weldon. "What Makes the Bible Unique?" *John Ankerberg Show* September 27, 2005. https://jashow.org/articles/what-makes-the-bible-unique/.

Answers in Genesis. "Faith in the Multiverse." July 23, 2011. https://answersingenesis.org/astronomy/cosmology/faith-in-the-multiverse/.

———. "Intelligent Design." https://answersingenesis.org/intelligent-design/.

———. "'Science vs. Religion' Argument 12." November 20, 2018. https://answersingenesis.org/apologetics/science-vs-religion/.

Ayyar, Kamakshi. "Understanding the Technology behind 3D Movies." *Firstpost (Tech 2)* February 25, 2010. https://www.firstpost.com/tech/news-analysis/understanding-the-technology-behind-3d-movies-3571505.html.

Barnhardt, Adam. "The Introduction of the Marvel Cinematic Multiverse—What It Means for Phase 4 and Beyond." *ComicBook* May 3, 2019. https://comicbook.com/marvel/news/marvel-cinematic-multiverse-what-it-means-for-phase-4/.

Bates, Gary. "*Designed* by Aliens?" *Creation* 25.4 (September 2003) 54–55. https://creation.com/designed-by-aliens-crick-watson-atheism-panspermia.

Batiz, Zoltán, and Bhag C. Chauhan. "Holographic Principle and Quantum Physics." *NeuroQuantology* 7.4 (December 2009) 665–76. https://neuroquantology.com/data-cms/articles/20191024120921pm260.pdf.

Beall, Abigail. "Theory Claims to Offer the First 'Evidence' Our Universe Is a Hologram." *Wired UK* January 31, 2017. http://www.wired.co.uk/article/our-universe-is-a-hologram.

Bibliography

Beekes, Robert. "κόσμος." In *Etymological Dictionary of Greek*, Vol. 1, 760. Leiden: Brill, 2010.

Behe, Michael J. *Darwin Devolves: The New Science about DNA That Challenges Evolution.* New York: HarperOne, 2019.

———. *Darwin's Black Box: The Biochemical Challenge to Evolution.* New York: Free Press, 2003.

Bergman, Jerry. "Wernher von Braun: The Father of Space Flight." *Institute for Creation Research* December 30, 2014. https://www.icr.org/article/wernher-von-braun-father-space-flight.

Bible Hub. "1819. damah." https://biblehub.com/hebrew/1819.htm.

———. "1892. hebel." https://biblehub.com/hebrew/1892.htm.

———. "'ă·ḏam·meh-." https://biblehub.com/hebrew/adammeh_1819.htm.

Bohra, Neelam, and AJ Willingham. "'WitchTok': Amid Uncertainty, a New Fascination with Astrology and the Occult Bubbles Up." *CNN* August 19, 2021. https://www.cnn.com/2021/08/19/us/witchtok-astrology-covid-19-pandemic-trnd/index.html.

Boudreaux, Richard. "World Religious Leaders Join Pope in a Peace Prayer." *Los Angeles Times* January 25, 2002. https://www.latimes.com/archives/la-xpm-2002-jan-25-mn-24702-story.html.

Boyle, Robert. "A Disquisition about the Final Causes of Natural Things." In *The Works of the Honourable Robert Boyle. In Five Volumes. To Which is Prefixed the Life of the Author*, Vol. 4, edited by Thomas Birch, 515–55. London: Andrew Millar, 1744.

Bradley, Bill. "The MCU Just Supported Every Phase 4 Multiverse Theory and Rumor." *ScreenRant* October 3, 2021. https://screenrant.com/mcu-marvel-phase-4-multiverse-rumors-theories-true/.

Bucklin, Stephanie Margaret. "Is the Multiverse Physics, Philosophy, or Something Else Entirely?" *Astronomy* January 18, 2017. https://astronomy.com/news/2017/01/what-is-the-multiverse.

Camp, Justin. "6 Christian Astronauts Who Trusted Science and God." *Crosswalk* April 21, 2020. https://www.crosswalk.com/faith/men/astronauts-who-trusted-science-and-god.html.

Carr, Bernard, ed. *Universe or Multiverse?* Cambridge: Cambridge University Press, 2007.

Catholic Online. "A Prayer for World Peace (Prayer for World Peace, 1978)." https://www.catholic.org/prayers/prayer.php?p=1506.

Chappell, Bill. "World's Muslim Population Will Surpass Christians This Century, Pew Says." *NPR* April 2, 2015. https://www.npr.org/sections/thetwo-way/2015/04/02/397042004/muslim-population-will-surpass-christians-this-century-pew-says.

The Character Quotes. "Cypher Quotes in The Matrix (1999)." https://www.thecharacterquotes.com/cypher.

Chery, Fritz. "Predestination vs. Free Will." *Bible Reasons* December 10, 2020. https://biblereasons.com/predestination-vs-free-will/.

Chretien, Claire. "Church Will Offer Catholics Plenary Indulgence for Attending 2018 March for Life." *LifeSiteNews* December 2, 2017. https://www.lifesitenews.com/news/plenary-indulgence-available-to-catholics-attending-the-2018-march-for-life/.

CNA. "'Galileo and the Vatican' Debunks Black Legend about Scientist and the Church." *Catholic News Agency* April 20, 2009. https://www.catholicnewsagency.com/news/galileo_and_the_vatican_debunks_black_legend_about_scientist_and_the_church.

Compelling Truth. "What Is the Theological Concept of Middle Knowledge?" https://www.compellingtruth.org/middle-knowledge.html.

Bibliography

Compendio, Chris. "The Multiverse Will Ruin the MCU." *The Escapist* May 29, 2019. https://www.escapistmagazine.com/the-multiverse-will-ruin-the-mcu/.

Copan, Paul. *True for You, but Not for Me: Deflating the Slogans that Leave Christians Speechless*. Minneapolis: Bethany House, 1998.

Craig, William Lane. "#157 Molinism vs. Calvinism." *Reasonable Faith* April 19, 2010. https://www.reasonablefaith.org/question-answer/P130/molinism-vs.-calvinism.

———. *The Cosmological Argument from Plato to Leibniz*. Eugene, OR: Wipf and Stock, 2001.

Cramer, John G. "The Other 40 Dimensions." *Analog Science Fiction and Fact Magazine* October 1, 1984. https://www.npl.washington.edu/AV/altvw06.html.

Crandell, Ben. "What the Long Island Medium Has Learned about Afterlife and Death during COVID." *South Florida Sun Sentinel* March 30, 2021. https://www.sun-sentinel.com/entertainment/theater-and-arts/fl-et-long-island-medium-interview-fort-lauderdale-broward-center-20210330-dl4gcgw2fbdwnlges54zmfc3za-story.html.

Crick, Francis. *Life Itself: Its Origin and Nature*. New York: Simon and Schuster, 1981.

Crowe, Brandon. "Not One Jot or Tittle." *Ligonier Ministries* September 25, 2015. https://www.ligonier.org/learn/articles/not-one-jot-or-tittle/.

Cuozzo, Jack. *Buried Alive: The Startling Truth about Neanderthal Man*. Green Forest, AR: Master, 1998.

Daily Mail. "How Jesus Is Most Famous Person in History . . . and Cameron Is Only 1,483rd, According to Internet Searches." *Daily Mail* December 14, 2013. https://www.dailymail.co.uk/news/article-2523930/Jesus-famous-person-history-according-software-algorithm.html.

Dao, Christine. "Man of Science, Man of God: George Washington Carver." *Institute for Creation Research* December 1, 2008. https://www.icr.org/article/science-man-god-george-washington-carver/.

Deem, Rich. "Predestination vs. Free Will—Is It One or the Other?" *Evidence for God* February 28, 2008. http://godandscience.org/doctrine/predestination.html.

Dhooper, Gaurav. "The AI Trajectory—Fear of Singularity." *Robotics Tomorrow* February 19, 2020. https://www.roboticstomorrow.com/article/2020/02/the-ai-trajectory-fear-of-singularity/14849.

Dodson, Aaron. "The Strange Legacy of Tupac's 'Hologram' Lives on Five Years After Its Historic Coachella Debut." *The Undefeated* April 14, 2017. https://theundefeated.com/features/the-strange-legacy-of-tupacs-hologram-after-coachella/.

Doyle, Shaun. "Plato and Christianity." *Creation Ministries International* April 30, 2016. https://creation.com/plato-and-christianity.

Easton, Matthew George. "Tittle." In *Easton's Bible Dictionary*, 3rd ed. London: Thomas Nelson, 1897. https://archive.org/details/EastonsBibleDictionary/page/n1159/mode/2up.

Eisenberg, Eric. "How Marvel's Multiverse Might Affect the MCU Going Forward." *Cinema Blend* November 10, 2016. https://www.cinemablend.com/news/1583720/how-marvels-multiverse-might-affect-the-mcu-going-forward.

Ellicott, Charles John, ed. *Ellicott's Commentary for English Readers*. London: Cassell and Co., 1905. https://biblehub.com/commentaries/ellicott/.

Elvy, Craig. "Predicting The Matrix 4's REAL Title—Why It Should Break the Rules." *ScreenRant* May 9, 2020. https://screenrant.com/matrix-4-title-prediction-resurrections-rebooted-different-reason/.

Bibliography

D'Emilio, Frances. "Pope Gives Final Absolution to Galileo." *Associated Press* October 31, 1992. https://apnews.com/0f3faa3ef29f5784d137a0d8c399e29e.

Episcopal Relief & Development. "A Prayer for Peace." https://www.episcopalrelief.org/prayer/prayer-for-peace/.

Erion, Gerald J., and Barry Smith. "Skepticism, Morality, and *The Matrix*." In *The Matrix and Philosophy: Welcome to the Desert of the Real*, edited by William Irwin, 16–27. Chicago: Open Court, 2002.

Europlanet Media Centre. "Could Life Have Survived a Fall to Earth?" *ScienceDaily* September 12, 2013. https://www.sciencedaily.com/releases/2013/09/130912092731.htm.

Fahle, John Joseph. *Galileo: His Life and Work*. New York: J. Pott, 1903.

Fahmy, Dalia. "Key Findings about Americans' Belief in God." *Pew Research Center* April 25, 2018. https://www.pewresearch.org/fact-tank/2018/04/25/key-findings-about-americans-belief-in-god/.

Faraday, Michael. *Experimental Researches in Chemistry and Physics*. London: R. Taylor and W. Francis, 1859.

Farrell-Vega, Jett. "Could Disney's Multiverse Craze Solve the Biggest Problems for Marvel and Star Wars in Their Parks?" *Theme Park Tourist* November 3, 2021. https://www.themeparktourist.com/features/20211103/32045/could-disneys-multiverse-craze-solve-biggest-problems-marvel-and-star-wars.

Faulkner, Danny R. "The Misplaced Faith of Isaac Newton." *Answers in Genesis* February 25, 2018. https://answersingenesis.org/creation-scientists/misplaced-faith-isaac-newton/.

Federer, William J. *George Washington Carver: His Life and Faith in His Own Words*. St. Louis: Amerisearch, 2003.

Fischer, Russ. "The 50 Greatest Sci-Fi Films of All Time." *Thrillist* January 4, 2018. https://www.thrillist.com/entertainment/nation/best-sci-fi-movies-of-all-time-ranked.

Folger, Tim. "Science's Alternative to an Intelligent Creator: The Multiverse Theory." *Discover Magazine* November 10, 2008. https://www.discovermagazine.com/the-sciences/sciences-alternative-to-an-intelligent-creator-the-multiverse-theory.

Frank, Adam. "What If Life on Earth Didn't Start on Earth?" *NPR* December 15, 2017. https://www.npr.org/sections/13.7/2017/12/15/571122951/what-if-life-on-earth-didn-t-start-on-earth.

Fuge, Jon. "Why Cypher Made the Right Choice in The Matrix According to Joe Pantoliano." *MovieWeb* April 29, 2020. https://movieweb.com/the-matrix-cypher-joe-pantoliano/.

Ganz, Jacob. "How That Tupac Hologram at Coachella Worked." *NPR* April 17, 2012. https://www.npr.org/sections/therecord/2012/04/17/150820261/how-that-tupac-hologram-at-coachella-worked.

Glattfelder, James B. "A Universe Built of Information." In *Information—Consciousness—Reality*, 13.4.2. Cham, Switzerland: Springer, 2019.

Godawa, Brian. "The Matrix: Unloaded Revelations." *Christian Research Institute* June 9, 2009. https://www.equip.org/article/the-matrix-unloaded-revelations/.

Got Questions Ministries. "Does Everyone Have a 'God-Shaped Hole'?" https://www.gotquestions.org/God-shaped-hole.html.

———. "Do Faith in God and Science Contradict?" https://www.gotquestions.org/science-God.html.

———. "What Does the Bible Say about Predestination vs. Free Will?" https://www.gotquestions.org/predestination-vs-free-will.html.

———. "What Is a Jot? What Is a Tittle?" https://www.gotquestions.org/jot-tittle.html.

Bibliography

———. "What Is Christian Gnosticism?" https://www.gotquestions.org/Christian-gnosticism.html.

Grace to You. "Ezekiel." https://www.gty.org/library/Bible-Introductions/MSB26/Ezekiel.

———. "Philippians." https://www.gty.org/library/bible-introductions/MSB50/philippians.

Graves, Dan. *Scientists of Faith: 48 Biographies of Historic Scientists and Their Christian Faith*. Grand Rapids: Kregel, 1996.

Greene, Brian. *The Hidden Reality: Parallel Universes and the Deep Laws of the Cosmos*. New York: Alfred A. Knopf, 2011.

———. "Our Universe May Be a Giant Hologram." *Discover Magazine* August 3, 2011. https://www.discovermagazine.com/technology/our-universe-may-be-a-giant-hologram.

Greene, Heather. "Study: Gen Z Doubles Down on Spirituality, Combining Tarot and Traditional Faith." *Religion News Service* August 11, 2021. https://religionnews.com/2021/08/11/study-gen-z-doubles-down-on-spirituality-combining-tarot-and-traditional-faith/.

Guan, Frank. "Why Ever Stop Playing Video Games." *Vulture* February 20, 2017. https://www.vulture.com/2017/02/video-games-are-better-than-real-life.html.

Haarsma, Deborah. "Universe or Multiverse, God Is Still the Creator." *Biologos* May 3, 2018. https://biologos.org/articles/universe-or-multiverse-god-is-still-the-creator.

Harrison, Mark. "What Went Wrong with The Matrix Sequels?" *Den of Geek* November 5, 2019. https://www.denofgeek.com/movies/what-went-wrong-with-the-matrix-sequels/.

Hawking, Stephen W., and Thomas Hertog. "A Smooth Exit from Eternal Inflation?" *Journal of High Energy Physics* 4 (2018). https://arxiv.org/abs/1707.07702.

Hayward, Alan. *Creation and Evolution*. Minneapolis: Bethany House, 1985.

Heritage, Stuart. "The Matrix: No 13 Best Sci-Fi and Fantasy Film of All Time." *The Guardian* October 21, 2010. https://www.theguardian.com/film/2010/oct/21/matrix-wachowskis-science-fiction.

Hodge, Ian. "The Cosmological Argument Needs the Law of Causality." *Journal of Creation* 28.1 (2014) 18–21.

Holographic Studios. "Interference Can Stop Things." https://www.holographer.com/interference/.

Hooper, Rowan. "Are There Multiple Universes?" *New Scientist*. https://www.newscientist.com/question/are-there-multiple-universes/.

———. "Hugh Everett: The Man Who Gave Us the Multiverse." *New Scientist* September 24, 2014. https://www.newscientist.com/article/dn26261-hugh-everett-the-man-who-gave-us-the-multiverse/.

———. "Multiverse Me: Should I Care about My Other Selves?" *New Scientist* September 24, 2014. https://www.newscientist.com/article/mg22329880-400-multiverse-me-should-i-care-about-my-other-selves/.

Horn, Thomas, and Cris Putnam. *Exo Vaticana: Petrus Romanus, Project L.U.C.I.F.E.R. and the Vatican's Astonishing Plan for the Arrival of an Alien Savior*. Crane, MO: Defender, 2013.

Huddleston, Tom, and Phil de Semlyen. "The 100 Best Sci-Fi Movies." *TimeOut* June 3, 2021. https://www.timeout.com/london/film/the-100-best-sci-fi-movies.

Hutchings, David. "Rewatching 'Spider-Verse': A Theological Response to the Possibility of a Multiverse." *Christianity Today* March 27, 2020. https://www.christianitytoday.com/ct/2020/march-web-only/spider-verse-hawking-theological-response-multiverse.html.

Bibliography

Hvistendahl, Mara. "Can We Stop AI Outsmarting Humanity?" *The Guardian* March 28, 2019. https://www.theguardian.com/technology/2019/mar/28/can-we-stop-robots-outsmarting-humanity-artificial-intelligence-singularity.

Illing, Sean. "Are We Living in a Computer Simulation? I Don't Know. Probably." *Vox* April 18, 2019. https://www.vox.com/future-perfect/2019/4/10/18275618/simulation-hypothesis-matrix-rizwan-virk.

IMDb. "The Matrix Resurrections." https://www.imdb.com/title/tt10838180/.

———. "Patrick Stewart: Capt. Jean-Luc Picard—The Big Goodbye (1988)—Star Trek: The Next Generation." https://www.imdb.com/title/tt0708787/characters/nm0001772.

James-Griffiths, Paul. "Eighteenth and Nineteenth Centuries." *Christian Heritage Edinburgh* August 11, 2016. https://www.christianheritageedinburgh.org.uk/2016/08/11/eighteenth-and-nineteenth-centuries/?utm_source=rss&utm_medium=rss&utm_campaign=eighteenth-and-nineteenth-centuries.

Jammer, Max. *Concepts of Simultaneity: From Antiquity to Einstein and Beyond.* Baltimore: Johns Hopkins University Press, 2006.

Jaradat, Mya. "Gen Z's Looking for Religion. You'd Be Surprised Where They Find It." *Deseret News* September 13, 2020. https://www.deseret.com/indepth/2020/9/13/21428404/gen-z-religion-spirituality-social-justice-black-lives-matter-parents-family-pandemic.

Jewish Virtual Library. "Jewish Concepts: The Name of God." https://www.jewishvirtuallibrary.org/the-name-of-god.

Josh McDowell Ministry. "Bible is Unique." https://www.josh.org/resurrection/bible-is-unique/.

Kac, Eduardo. "Photonic Webs in Time: The Art of Holography." http://www.ekac.org/photonic.Webs.ISEA_95.html.

Kaku, Michio. *Parallel Worlds: A Journey through Creation, Higher Dimensions, and the Future of the Cosmos.* New York: Anchor, 2004.

Karr, Rick. "The Spiritual Message of 'The Matrix.'" *NPR* May 16, 2003. https://www.npr.org/templates/story/story.php?storyId=1264976.

Katholieke Universiteit Leuven. ". . . the rest are details, Einstein 1905–2005." http://itf.fys.kuleuven.be/~christ/pub/ENposters.pdf.

Kaufman, Gil. "Exclusive: Tupac Coachella Hologram Source Explains How Rapper Resurrected." *MTV* April 16, 2012. http://www.mtv.com/news/1683173/tupac-hologram-coachella/.

Kaufman, Marc. "Did Life on Earth Come from Mars?" *National Geographic* September 5, 2013. https://www.nationalgeographic.com/news/2013/9/130905-mars-origin-of-life-earth-panspermia-astrobiology/.

Kennedy, Graham, and Ian Kennedy. "The Holodeck." *Daystrom Institute Technical Library* April 20, 2020. http://www.ditl.org/article-page.php?ArticleID=45&ListID=Articles.

Kinder, Lucy. "Do We Live in the Matrix? Scientists Believe They May Have Answered the Question." *Telegraph* November 20, 2013. https://www.telegraph.co.uk/news/science/science-news/10451983/Do-we-live-in-the-Matrix-Scientists-believe-they-may-have-answered-the-question.html.

Klinghoffer, David. "Another Problem with Panspermia." *Evolution News* October 16, 2012. https://evolutionnews.org/2012/10/another_problem_1/.

Bibliography

Koberlein, Brian. "Evidence for the Strange Idea that the Universe Is a Hologram." *Nautilus* February 21, 2017. http://nautil.us/blog/new-evidence-for-the-strange-idea-that-the-universe-is-a-hologram.

Kriss, Sam. "The Multiverse Idea Is Rotting Culture." *The Atlantic* August 29, 2016. https://www.theatlantic.com/science/archive/2016/08/the-multiverse-as-imagination-killer/497417/.

Kuhn, Robert Lawrence. "Confronting the Multiverse: What 'Infinite Universes' Would Mean." *Space.com* December 23, 2015. https://www.space.com/31465-is-our-universe-just-one-of-many-in-a-multiverse.html.

Kurzweil, Ray. "Questions and Answers." *Singularity.com*. http://www.singularity.com/qanda.html.

Lamont, Ann. *21 Great Scientists Who Believed the Bible*. Acacia Ridge, Australia: Creation Science Foundation, 1995.

———. "Sir Isaac Newton (1642/3–1727)." *Answers in Genesis* June 1, 1990. https://answersingenesis.org/creation-scientists/profiles/sir-isaac-newton/.

Lawlor, Kevin. "10 Reasons The Matrix Sequels Are Worth While." *ComingSoon* March 31, 2019. https://www.comingsoon.net/movies/features/1022403-10-reasons-the-matrix-sequels-are-worth-while.

Lennox, John. *Against the Flow: The Inspiration of Daniel in an Age of Relativism*. Chicago: Lion Hudson, 2015.

———. *Can Science Explain Everything?* Epsom, UK: The Good Book, 2019.

Lewis, C. S. *Mere Christianity*. New York: Simon and Schuster, 1996.

———. *Miracles: A Preliminary Study*. Grand Rapids: Baker, 1969.

———. *The Weight of Glory and Other Addresses*. New York: Macmillan, 1949.

Lexico. "Virtual." https://www.lexico.com/en/definition/virtual.

Libbey, Dirk. "30 Best Sci-Fi Movies of All Time." *Cinema Blend* June 9, 2017. https://www.cinemablend.com/news/1639139/30-best-sci-fi-movies-of-all-time.

Liddell, Henry George, et al., eds. *A Greek-English Lexicon*. 9th ed. Oxford: Clarendon, 1940.

Ligonier Ministries. "The First and Primary Cause." March 31, 2017. https://www.ligonier.org/learn/devotionals/first-and-primary-cause/.

Lincoln, Don. "Einstein's Quest to 'Know God's Thoughts' Could Take Millennia." *Live Science* June 4, 2019. https://www.livescience.com/65628-theory-of-everything-millennia-away.html.

Lisle, Jason. "Does Science Need God?" *Answers in Genesis* April 3, 2009. https://answersingenesis.org/what-is-science/does-science-need-god/.

———. "How Do I Know that I Know?—A Response (Part 2)." *Biblical Science Institute* September 11, 2020. https://biblicalscienceinstitute.com/apologetics/how-do-i-know-that-i-know-a-response-part-2/.

Long, Tony. "Sept. 11, 1822: Church Admits It's Not All about Us." *Wired UK* September 10, 2000. https://www.wired.com/2008/09/sept-11-1822-church-admits-its-not-all-about-us-2/.

Lubenow, Martin L. *Bones of Contention: A Creationist Assessment of Human Fossils*. Grand Rapids: Baker, 1992.

Lubotsky, Alexander. "The Indo-European Suffix *-ens-* and Its Indo-European Origin." In *The Precursors of Proto-Indo-European: The Indo-Anatolian and Indo-Uralic Hypotheses*, edited by A. Kloekhorst and T. Pronk, 151–62. Leiden: Brill, 2019.

Bibliography

Macdonald, Fleur. "What, If Anything, Can Psychics Tell Us about All of This?" *New York Times* January 15, 2021. https://www.nytimes.com/2021/01/15/style/did-you-predict-this.html.

McGee, J. Vernon. *Philippians–Colossians: Thru the Bible Commentary Series*. Nashville: Thomas Nelson, 1995.

Marlowe, Michael. "What Is Arminianism?" *Bible Research*. http://www.bible-researcher.com/arminianism.html.

Marshall, Rick. "How Disney Could (and Should) Bring the X-Men into the Marvel Cinematic Universe." *Digital Trends* July 24, 2019. https://www.digitaltrends.com/movies/x-men-in-marvel-cinematic-universe/.

Marshall, Rick, and Nick Perry. "The Matrix Resurrections: Everything We Know about the Upcoming Matrix Sequel." *Digital Trends* September 10, 2021. https://www.digitaltrends.com/movies/matrix-4-release-date-news-cast-trailer/.

Martin, Walter. *The Kingdom of the Cults*. Edited by Hank Hanegraff. Minneapolis: Bethany House, 1997.

The Marvel Cinematic Universe Wiki. "Stan Lee." *Fandom*. https://marvelcinematicuniverse.fandom.com/wiki/Stan_Lee.

Mathison, Keith A. "Are the Bible and Science Compatible?" *Tabletalk Magazine* 53 (August 2017) 24–25. https://tabletalkmagazine.com/article/2017/08/are-the-bible-and-science-compatible/.

———. "Luther, Calvin, and Copernicus—A Reformed Approach to Science and Scripture." *Ligonier Ministries* June 1, 2012. https://www.ligonier.org/blog/luther-calvin-and-copernicus-reformed-approach-science-and-scripture/.

The Matrix Wiki. "Cypherites." *Fandom*. https://matrix.fandom.com/wiki/Cypherites.

Memory Alpha. "The Big Goodbye (Episode)." *Fandom*. https://memory-alpha.fandom.com/wiki/The_Big_Goodbye_(episode).

———. "Holodeck." *Fandom*. https://memory-alpha.fandom.com/wiki/Holodeck.

Merali, Zeeya. "Do We Live in the Matrix?" *Discover Magazine* November 14, 2013. https://www.discovermagazine.com/the-sciences/do-we-live-in-the-matrix.

Merriam-Webster Online. "Entropy." https://www.merriam-webster.com/dictionary/entropy.

———. "Hologram." https://www.merriam-webster.com/dictionary/hologram.

———. "Information." https://www.merriam-webster.com/dictionary/information.

———. "Materialism." https://www.merriam-webster.com/dictionary/materialism.

Meyer, Stephen C. "How Christianity Gave Rise to Modern Science." *Crossway* December 13, 2017. https://www.crossway.org/articles/how-christianity-gave-rise-to-modern-science/.

Miller, Jeff. "The Anthropic Principle: The Universe Is Designed for Us." *Apologetics Press* October 21, 2018. https://apologeticspress.org/the-anthropic-principle-the-universe-is-designed-for-us-5619/.

———. "The Law of Causality and the Uncaused Cause." *Apologetics Press* November 25, 2012. http://apologeticspress.org/apcontent.aspx?category=12&article=1601.

Minkel. J. R. "Sidebar: The Holographic Principle." *Scientific American* April 7, 2003. https://www.scientificamerican.com/article/sidebar-the-holographic-p/.

Missler, Chuck. "A Message from Outside Time." *Koinonia House* June 1, 2013. https://www.khouse.org/articles/2013/1123/.

———. "Quantum Physics: The Boundaries of Reality." *Koinonia House* July 1, 1998. https://www.khouse.org/articles/1998/62/.

Bibliography

———. *Supplemental Notes: The Book of Ezekiel*. Coeur d'Alene, ID: Koinonia House, 2008.
Missler, Chuck, and Mark Eastman. *Alien Encounters: The Secret behind the UFO Phenomenon*. Coeur d'Alene, ID: Koinonia House, 1997.
Moffat, John W. *Cracking the Particle Code of the Universe: The Hunt for the Higgs Boson*. Oxford: Oxford University Press, 2013.
———. "Taking the Multiverse on Faith." *Physics World* April 20, 2011. https://physicsworld.com/a/taking-the-multiverse-on-faith/.
Morris, Henry M. "Bible-Believing Scientists of the Past." *Institute for Creation Research* January 1, 1982. https://www.icr.org/article/bible-believing-scientists-past.
———. *Men of Science, Men of God*. Green Forest, AR: Master, 1982.
———. *Scientific Creationism*. Green Forest, AR: Master, 1974.
Morris, John D. "Does Science Conflict with the Bible?" *Institute of Creation Research* November 1, 1997. https://www.icr.org/article/1173/.
Moskowitz, Clara. "Controversially, Physicist Argues Time Is Real." *Live Science* April 26, 2013. https://www.livescience.com/29081-time-real-illusion-smolin.html.
———. "String Theory May Create Far Fewer Universes Than Thought." *Live Science* July 30, 2018. https://www.livescience.com/63204-string-theory-multiverse.html.
Mulfinger, George, and Julia Mulfinger Orozco. *Christian Men of Science: Eleven Men Who Changed the World*. Greenville, SC: Ambassador International, 2004.
Murphy, Jason. "The Matrix (Movie Review)." *Christian Answers*. https://christiananswers.net/spotlight/movies/pre2000/i-thematrix.html.
Musumeci, Natalie. "Witches around the World Plot Mass Spell against Trump." *New York Post* February 24, 2017. https://nypost.com/2017/02/24/witches-around-the-world-plot-mass-spell-against-trump/.
Neller, Ron. "Do You Know the Laws of the Heavens?" *Journal of Creation* 28.3 (December 2014) 61–66. https://creation.com/the-bible-and-the-hydrologic-cycle.
New Scientist. *The Quantum World: The Disturbing Theory at the Heart of Reality*. London: John Murray Learning, 2017.
Newton, Isaac. *The Mathematical Principles of Natural Philosophy*. Edited by N. W. Chittenden. Translated by Andrew Motte. New York: Daniel Adee, 1846.
Oikoumene World Council of Churches. "Church and Ecumenical Relations." https://www.oikoumene.org/what-we-do/church-and-ecumenical-relations.
Orlic, Christian. "The Origins of Directed Panspermia." *Scientific American* January 9, 2013. https://blogs.scientificamerican.com/guest-blog/the-origins-of-directed-panspermia/.
Oxford Reference. "Phlogiston theory." https://www.oxfordreference.com/view/10.1093/oi/authority.20110803100323514.
Parsons, Gradye. "PC(USA) Stated Clerk Responds to Ferguson Grand Jury Decision." *PC(USA)* November 24, 2014. https://www.pcusa.org/news/2014/11/24/pcusa-stated-clerk-responds-ferguson-grand-jury/.
Pascal, Blaise. *Pascal's Pensées*. Translated by William Finlayson Trotter. New York: E. P. Dutton, 1958.
Patel, Tara. "Vatican Admits Galileo Was Right." *New Scientist* November 7, 1992. https://www.newscientist.com/article/mg13618460-600-vatican-admits-galileo-was-right/.
Patton, Michael. "The Danger of Sola Scriptura." *Bible.org* October 3, 2005. https://bible.org/article/danger-sola-scriptura.

Bibliography

Perez, Isabel Yarwood. "Holograms: Blurring the Lines of Reality." *Illumin Magazine* January 31, 2020. https://illumin.usc.edu/holograms-blurring-the-lines-of-reality/.

Rader, Dotson. "The Mixed-Up Life of Shia LaBeouf." *Parade* June 14, 2009. https://parade.com/130832/dotsonrader/shia-labeouf-mixed-up-life/.

Rajaram, Dhiraj, Krishna Rupanagunta, and Aditya Kumbakonem. "Data Assets: Information Decay." *Analytics Magazine* (March/April 2014) 30–33. https://pubsonline.informs.org/do/10.1287/LYTX.2014.02.02/full/.

Ratner, Paul. "New Hypothesis Argues the Universe Simulates Itself into Existence." *Big Think* April 26, 2020. https://bigthink.com/surprising-science/new-hypothesis-argues-the-universe-simulates-itself-into-existence?rebelltitem=4#rebelltitem4.

Reddit. "Outside: The Free-To-Play MMO, on Reddit." https://reddit.com/r/outside.

Regis, Edward. *What Is Life? Investigating the Nature of Life in the Age of Synthetic Biology*. New York: Farrar, Straus and Giroux, 2008.

Reichenbach, Bruce. "Cosmological Argument." *The Stanford Encyclopedia of Philosophy*, edited by Edward N. Zalta. https://plato.stanford.edu/entries/cosmological-argument/.

Ross, Hugh. "Anthropic Principle: A Precise Plan for Humanity." *Reasons to Believe* January 1, 2002. https://reasons.org/explore/publications/facts-for-faith/read/facts-for-faith/2002/01/01/anthropic-principle-a-precise-plan-for-humanity.

Salaman, Esther. "A Talk with Einstein." *The Listener* 54 (1955) 370–71.

Schaefer, Sandy. "The Flash: DCEU Multiverse Is Copying the Arrowverse Model." *ScreenRant* August 24, 2020. https://screenrant.com/flash-dceu-multiverse-copy-arrowverse-crisis-infinite-earths-explained/.

Scholes, Sarah. "Can Physicists Ever Prove the Multiverse Is Real?" *Smithsonian Magazine* April 19, 2016. https://www.smithsonianmag.com/science-nature/can-physicists-ever-prove-multiverse-real-180958813/.

Schulze-Makuch, Dirk. "Reaching the Singularity May be Humanity's Greatest and Last Accomplishment." *Air and Space Magazine* March 27, 2020. https://www.airspacemag.com/daily-planet/reaching-singularity-may-be-humanitys-greatest-and-last-accomplishment-180974528/.

Shea, William, and Marinao Artigas. *Galileo in Rome: The Rise and Fall of a Troublesome Genius*. Oxford: Oxford University Press, 2003.

Siegfried, Tom. "Making Sense of Many Universes." *Knowable Magazine* April 26, 2018. https://knowablemagazine.org/article/physical-world/2018/making-sense-many-universes.

Sims, David. "*The Matrix 4* Could Be Just What Hollywood Needs." *The Atlantic* August 21, 2019. https://www.theatlantic.com/entertainment/archive/2019/08/matrix-sequel-confirmed-lana-wachowski-keanu-reeves/596512/.

Singh-Kurtz, Sangeeta, and Dan Kopf. "The US Witch Population Has Seen an Astronomical Rise." *Quartz Media* October 4, 2018. https://qz.com/quartzy/1411909/the-explosive-growth-of-witches-wiccans-and-pagans-in-the-us/.

Slick, Matt. "Cosmological Argument for God's Existence." *Christian Apologetics and Research Ministry* April 28, 2021. https://carm.org/cosmological-argument.

———. "If Predestination Is True, Then How Can There Be Free Will?" *Christian Apologetics and Research Ministry* December 1, 2008. https://carm.org/if-predestination-true-then-how-can-there-be-free-will.

———. "Is Christianity against Science?" *Christian Apologetics and Research Ministry* November 25, 2008. https://carm.org/christianity-and-science.

Bibliography

Smith, David M. "The Cost of Lost Data." *Graziadio Business Review* 6.3 (2003). https://gbr.pepperdine.edu/2010/08/the-cost-of-lost-data/.

Smolin, Lee. *Time Reborn: From the Crisis in Physics to the Future of the Universe*. Boston: Mariner, 2014.

Souders, Travis. "New Class Explores Philosophy through Video Games." *Chico State Today* October 15, 2019. https://today.csuchico.edu/philosophy-and-video-games/.

Speziali, Pierre, ed. *Albert Einstein, Michele Besso, Correspondence, 1903–1955*. Histoire de la Pensée 17. Paris: Hermann, 1972.

Star Trek: The Next Generation, season 1, episode 12, "The Big Goodbye." Directed by Joseph L. Scanlan. Aired January 11, 1988.

State of Delaware. "Statement in Observance of Christian Heritage Week." *Wallbuilders*. https://wallbuilders.com/chw/delaware/.

Stewart, Don. "Has Christianity Opposed the Advancement of Science?" *Blue Letter Bible*. https://www.blueletterbible.org/faq/don_stewart/don_stewart_606.cfm.

———. "Is There Any Biblical Support for Purgatory?" *Blue Letter Bible*. https://www.blueletterbible.org/faq/don_stewart/don_stewart_123.cfm.

———. "What Is the Roman Catholic Claim as to Where Ultimate Authority Resides?" *Blue Letter Bible*. https://www.blueletterbible.org/Comm/stewart_don/faq/bible-ultimate-authority/question4-roman-catholic-claim-ultimate-authority.cfm.

Stoljar, Daniel, "Physicalism." *The Stanford Encyclopedia of Philosophy*, edited by Edward N. Zalta. https://plato.stanford.edu/entries/physicalism/.

Stromberg, Joseph. "Some Physicists Believe We're Living in a Giant Hologram—and It's Not That Far-Fetched." *Vox* June 29, 2015. https://www.vox.com/2015/6/29/8847863/holographic-principle-universe-theory-physics.

Susskind, Leonard. "Black Holes and the Information Paradox." *Scientific American* 276.4 (April 1997) 52–57.

Sutter, Paul. "How the Universe Could Possibly Have More Dimensions." *Space.com* February 21, 2020. https://www.space.com/more-universe-dimensions-for-string-theory.html.

Thomas, Brian. "'Multiverse' Theory Fails to Explain Away God." *Institute for Creation Research* December 3, 2008. https://www.icr.org/article/multiverse-theory-fails-explain-away-god/.

Thompson, Silvanus P. *The Life of William Thomson, Baron Kelvin of Largs*. London: Macmillan, 1910.

Tingle, Mark. "The Logic of Phlogiston." *Royal Society of Chemistry* January 6, 2014. https://edu.rsc.org/feature/the-logic-of-phlogiston/2000126.article.

Tomorrow's World Today. "Becoming 3D: Holograms and the Entertainment Industry." May 10, 2018. https://www.tomorrowsworldtoday.com/2018/05/10/music-in-3d-the-rise-of-holograms-in-music/.

Tourjée, Diana. "Real Life Is Not Enough: On Choosing Virtual Reality over the Physical World." *Vice* July 14, 2016. https://www.vice.com/en/article/mgmmdv/real-life-is-not-enough-on-choosing-virtual-reality-over-the-physical-world.

United Nations Framework Convention on Climate Change (UNFCCC). "World Religious Leaders and Scientists Make Pre-COP26 Appeal." October 5, 2021. https://unfccc.int/news/world-religious-leaders-and-scientists-make-pre-cop26-appeal.

University of Cambridge (Research). "Taming the Multiverse: Stephen Hawking's Final Theory about the Big Bang." May 2, 2018. https://www.cam.ac.uk/research/news/taming-the-multiverse-stephen-hawkings-final-theory-about-the-big-bang.

Bibliography

Vaidman, Lev. "Many-Worlds Interpretation of Quantum Mechanics." *The Stanford Encyclopedia of Philosophy*, edited by Edward N. Zalta. https://plato.stanford.edu/archives/fall2021/entries/qm-manyworlds/.

Variety. "'Avengers: Endgame' Passes 'Avatar' to Become Biggest Movie in History." *NBC News* July 20, 2019. https://www.nbcnews.com/pop-culture/movies/avengers-endgame-passes-avatar-become-biggest-movie-history-n1032041.

Vatican Observatory. "The Galileo Affair." http://www.vaticanobservatory.va/content/specolavaticana/en/research/history-of-astronomy/the-galileo-affair.html.

Velázquez, Fernando. "Existence in a Hologram: What Is Reality?" *Wall Street International Magazine* October 24, 2017. https://wsimag.com/science-and-technology/31901-our-existence-in-a-hologram.

Wachowski, Larry, and Andy Wachowski, dirs. *The Matrix*. Burbank, CA: Warner Bros., 1999.

———. *The Matrix Reloaded*. Burbank, CA: Warner Bros., 2003.

———. *The Matrix Revolutions*. Burbank, CA: Warner Bros., 2003.

Walsh, Michael. "Everything You Need to Know about the MCU's Multiverse." *Nerdist* September 13, 2021. https://nerdist.com/article/marvel-multiverse-explained-doctor-strange-wandavision-loki-mcu/.

Waugh, Rob. "We Will Find Out the Universe Is a Hologram (and It Could Change Everything)." *Metro UK* June 14, 2019. https://metro.co.uk/2019/06/14/we-will-find-out-the-universe-is-a-hologram-and-it-could-change-everything-9945431/.

Whitney, E. Oliver. "15 Years Later, 'The Matrix Reloaded' Is Better Than You Remember." *ScreenCrush* May 15, 2018. https://screencrush.com/the-matrix-reloaded-15-anniversary-defense/.

Wieselman, Jarett. "The Man at the Center of DC's TV Multiverse." *BuzzFeed News* October 22, 2014. https://www.buzzfeednews.com/article/jarettwieselman/the-man-at-the-center-of-dcs-tv-multiverse.

Williams, Matt. "A Universe of 10 Dimensions." December 11, 2014. https://phys.org/news/2014-12-universe-dimensions.html.

Wilson, William. "Similitude." In *Wilson's Old Testament Word Studies*, 395. McLean, VA: MacDonald, 1990.

Winfield, Nicole. "Masked Pope, Faith Leaders Pray for Peace and Pandemic's End." *Associated Press* October 20, 2020. https://apnews.com/article/virus-outbreak-pandemics-italy-pope-francis-prayer-a8d05ce7f76b1eafc5abcf82acdeb876.

Wojnar, Jason. "The 5 Best (and 5 Worst) Things about the Matrix Sequels." *ScreenRant* July 16, 2019. https://screenrant.com/matrix-sequels-best-worst-things/.

Woodford, Chris. "Holograms." *Explain That Stuff!* November 17, 2020. https://www.explainthatstuff.com/holograms.html.

Workman, Robert. "What Is a Hologram?" *Live Science* May 13, 2013. https://www.livescience.com/34652-hologram.html.

World Population Review. "Countries That Celebrate Christmas." https://worldpopulationreview.com/country-rankings/countries-that-celebrate-christmas.

Zweerink, Jeff. "Multiverse Musings: How Does Inflation Lead to a Multiverse?" *Reasons to Believe* September 14, 2010. https://reasons.org/explore/publications/articles/multiverse-musings-how-does-inflation-lead-to-a-multiverse.

General Index

absolute truth, 12, 17, 40–41, 48–49, 77–79, 88
   and the multiverse, 118
agnosticism, 78, 104
   and the multiverse, 121
alternate realities, xv
   in fiction, 117–19
alternative selves, 118–19
alternative worlds *(see alternate realities)*
apologetics, 38, 98, 120, 122–23
Arminianism *(see free will)*
artificial intelligence (AI), 20, 22, 99, 103–4
atheism, 16, 102, 104–5, 123
Bible
   and scientific discovery, 16–17
   exclusivity of, 50–51, 98
   inerrancy and divine inspiration of, 12–13, 40–41, 47–49, 123
   patterns in, 32, 39–44
   prophecy, 39, 41, 98, 120
   study of, 12, 17, 50–51, 76, 89–90, 127
   uniqueness of, 47–49
   worldview of, xv, xviii, 12, 46, 50–51, 55, 89–90, 121–23
Bibleverse, xv, 33–34, 41
black hole, 3–6
Boyle, Robert, 14
von Braun, Wernher, 15

Buddhism, 97–98
Carver, George Washington, 15
Catholicism
   and Galileo (Galileo Incident), 10–12
   comparison with *sola scriptura* worldview, 12–13
cosmological argument, 101–2, 107
cosmology, 100–109
cosmos, 80
creation
   and deeper structure, 71–74
   as having an end, 56, 66–67, 74, 80, 86–88, 94, 107
   of non-material virtual worlds, 19–20
Crick, Francis, 105
data, 5
data corruption (information decay), 86–88, 94–95
DC (DCEU), xv, 111, 115–22
decay *(see also entropy)*
   of creation and information, xxii, 28, 31–32, 56–57, 61, 66, 86–89
   related to eternal death in hell, 56
design, xxii, 29
   and deception, 106–9
   God as Designer, 8–9, 17, 29, 40–47, 51, 80, 100–102, 108, 113–22
   of the holodeck, 25–27
   of the Matrix, 21–22, 99–100

General Index

dimensions, 1–7, 46, 63–65, 117–18
   and prophetic visions, 44–47
   four-dimensional (4D), 29, 43–44
   God's unlimited view, 74
   related to comic book multiverses, 113–21
   three-dimensional (3D), xvi–xvii, 1–7, 21, 29, 43–44, 63–65 (movie analogy), 103
   two-dimensional (2D), xvi–xvii, 2–7, 29, 43–44, 63–65 (storybook analogy), 71
ecumenicalism, 94
Einstein, Albert, 3, 16, 66
Elisha, 75–76
entropy, 3–4, 79, 107
eternal inflation, 112
eternity, 21–22, 29, 52–61, 71, 76, 90–91, 107–8
evidence
   related to Christian faith, 8–10, 17, 37–38, 98, 101–2, 106, 114–15, 120–23
evolution *(see also cosmology)*
   and problems of, 104–7
   and the multiverse, 113
extraterrestrials, 25, 46, 102–7
Ezekiel, 44–46
faith *(see also evidence)*, 8, 14–18, 37–38, 57–58, 76, 89, 122–23, 127
   and prayer, 91
   in Hebrews 11, 37–38, 52–53
   related to non-Biblical faith, 83–84, 98, 107, 114, 120–21, 124
fall of man, 4, 51–53, 66, 86–88
   and the curse, 52, 57, 89, 95
   and the multiverse, 121
Faraday, Michael, 14–15
Feige, Kevin, 116
free will (Arminianism), 67–71
Galilei, Galileo, 10–12
gamification *(see Outside)*
Gnosticism, 97–98
God-shaped hole, 51–52
Hawking, Stephen, 112–13, 118
heaven, 17, 33–36, 42–44, 47, 52, 71, 125–27

hell *(see also salvation)*, 33–34, 52, 56, 125–27
holiness
   conforming to Christ, 35, 49, 88–90
   God's permanence and purity, 45, 48–49, 58, 125
holodeck, 25–29
hologram *(see also holographic image)*, 17, 43–44, 63, 72–74, 89 (story analogy)
   defined, 1–2
   reality beyond, 37–38, 56, 94–95
holograph *(see also hologram, holographic image)*
   defined, 1–2
holographic image *(see also hologram)*, xvii
   and worldview, 64–65, 79
   as a shadow/copy, 41–43, 53, 56, 71–74, 94
   defined, 1–7, 64–65
   ending of, 32–33, 86–88, 94–95, 100–102
holographic principle *(see also holographic universe)*
   and perspective, 50–51, 89
   and worldview, 29, 32, 37–38, 46, 50–51, 64–66, 70, 74, 82, 96–98, 100–108, 122
   defined, 3–7, 63, 72
holographic universe *(see also hologram, holographic image)*, xvi–xviii
   and the multiverse, 112, 117, 121
   and worldview, 17, 32–34, 37–38, 50–51, 75, 77–82, 92, 96–98, 122
   as a shadow/copy, 43, 71–74
   as simulated universes in science fiction, 19–29
   daily relevance of, 28–29
   defined, 4–7, 63–64, 72
   origins *(see also cosmology)*, 99–100, 104–6, 109
   reality beyond, 60
hyperdimensional, 46
ideology, xv, 120
impermanence, xxii, 22, 31–33, 37, 49, 53–56, 73–74, 86–88

General Index

information, 41, 56, 82, 109
   and the holographic principle, 3–7 (mosaic analogy), 63–66, 72, 99–100
   and the Matrix, 5, 21–22
   decay, 86–88
   defined, 5
   related to the Bible as divine information *(see also Bible)*, 22, 40
   visible to God, 69–70
information theory, 100
Intelligent Design, 100–102, 113, 120–22
intentional/purposeful living, 34–36, 64
investment for eternity, 29, 36, 38, 56–59, 125
Isaiah, 44–47
Israel, xxi, 32, 59–61
   and problems of replacement theology, 92
Jesus Christ
   and Christian worldview, 38, 55–57, 67–71, 82, 84–85, 89–95, 98, 121–23
   as High Priest, 41–44
   as Savior, 21–22, 31, 33–34, 56–58, 79, 124–27
   in Biblical Christianity, 12–13
   interactions with disciples, 33
   origins beyond our reality, 46–49, 54–55, 59–62, 108
Jewish festivals, 41–43
laws of thermodynamics, 3–4, 15, 28–29, 32, 107
laws of relativity, 3, 66, 72
Lee, Stan, 116
Lewis, C. S., 17, 52
Marvel (MCU), 111–19, 121
materialism, 81–84, 97
The Matrix (franchise), 5, 20–29, 96–100
   and philosophy, 22–25, 96–100
   cultural reception of, 20–21, 96–97
Matrix, 5, 19–29
   and artificial intelligence/sentience, 99, 104
   and philosophy, 22–24, 96–100
   and the Bible, 21–22
   cultural reception of, 22–25
Missler, Chuck, 4, 46–47, 106

Molinism, 69–71
Mosaic Law, 41–44
multiverse, 104, 111–22
Nachmanides, 4
new heaven(s) and new earth, 86–87, 94–95
Newton, Isaac, 14
Outside subreddit *(see also video games)*, 24, 29
Paganism, 83–84
panconsciousness, 102–7
panspermia, 102–7
parallel worlds, 117–19
patterns
   in the Bible and prophecy, 32, 39–43
   of information, 6, 109
   of light, 2
perspective, 27, 64, 97–98, 121
   inside the hologram, xvi–xvii, 7, 41, 64–65, 74–76
   outside the hologram, 50–51, 63–66
Picard, Jean-Luc (Captain, *Star Trek: The Next Generation*), 26–27
photograph, 1–2, 71
phlogiston, 9
physics
   and the holographic principle, 3–4, 17–18, 28–29, 72, 100
   and time, 66
   in other universes, 101–2, 112–22
   laws of, 3–4, 12, 16, 28–29, 32
Plato, 55, 107
prayer, 90–94, 126–27
priesthood (of the Mosaic Law), 32, 41–44
   and Ezekiel, 45
prophecy *(see also patterns)*, xxi, 32–33, 39–40, 92
   and evidence, 98, 120
prophets, 39, 44–47
predestination (Calvinism), 67–71
reality, xvii, 17, 20, 29, 59, 64–65, 77–78, 82, 102–4, 107–9, 125–27
   and Christ, 53, 79, 84–85, 92–94
   and holograms, 1, 43, 71–74, 82
   and the Bible, 21, 31–38, 41, 43–45, 48, 65, 79, 88
   and the holodeck, 26–28

General Index

reality *(cont.)*
    and time, 66, 70
    and views of supernatural reality, 46–47, 75–76
    in *The Matrix* franchise, 5, 20–29, 97–100
    multiple realities, 111, 119, 121
    virtual realities, 19–29, 101, 107
relative truth, 77–79, 118
replacement theology, 92
rewards, 31–32, 34, 36, 56–59
salvation
    and the Matrix, 97
    and the multiverse, 121
    through Christ alone, 12, 33–34, 56–58, 92–93, 124–27
science, 17–18, 32, 72, 74, 78
    and absolute truth, 79
    and Christianity, xxi–xxiii, 8–10, 13–18, 44, 46, 74, 104, 121–22
    and the Matrix, 20
    discounted theories of, 9–12
    observation and development of, 9–10, 72, 101, 111–22
    untestable theories of, 120–22
science fiction *(see also DC, Marvel, The Matrix, Star Trek)*
    and the holographic universe, 1
    and science, xvii, 112
    cultural impact of, 23–25, 96–97, 111
self-actualization, 102–4
sentience *(see artificial intelligence)*
shadows, 41–44, 47, 56, 75, 79
Shakur, Tupac, 72–73
simulated realities, 5, 17, 19–29, 71, 74, 78, 96, 98–103, 107
simulation hypothesis, 20, 98–103
sin *(see also fall of man)*
    and humans' fallen nature, 7, 13, 48, 51, 54, 57–58, 84, 87–89, 104

    and need for salvation, 22, 34, 53–55, 79, 87, 89, 91, 97, 125–27
    as corrupting the universe *(see also data corruption)*, 66, 86–88
    as distinct from holiness, 48, 77, 89
singularity hypothesis, 103–4
social justice, 82, 92–95
sola scriptura, 12–13
spacetime, 65 (bubble analogy), 74, 102–4
    and the multiverse, 111, 118
spiritual growth, 34–36, 49–51, 84, 88–92, 123, 127
spiritual warfare, 46, 75, 84, 106
spiritualism, 83–85, 96–98
Star Trek, 25–29
string theory, 4, 43–44, 111–12
supernatural, 33, 41–45, 75–76, 105–6
    American belief in, 83–84
Tabernacle, 32, 41–45, 53–56
    of earthly bodies as tabernacles, 54
Temple, 42, 44–45
    First (Solomon's), 45
    Third, xxi
theory of everything, 16
theory of forms, 107
theory of relativity, 3–4, 66, 72
Thomson, William (Lord Kelvin), 15
time, 4, 29, 63–65, 71–72, 86
    and the multiverse, 111
    as a measurement, 65–67, 71
    in virtual/simulated realities, 5, 28
    related to timelessness of God and the Bible, 44, 47, 51, 60–61, 69–71, 74, 108
timeless emergentism, 102–3
UFOs *(see also extraterrestrials)*, 46
universal illusions, 19–22, 28–29, 72, 96–103
video games, 23–25
virtual worlds, 19–29, 96–100
Wiccanism, 83–84

Scripture Index

OLD TESTAMENT

Genesis
1	80, 108
1:1–2	108
1:3	80
1:6	80
1:9	80
1:11	80
1:14	80
1:20	80
1:22	80
1:24	80
1:26	80
1:28	80
1:29	80
2:7	107
3	4, 51, 53, 86
11	94

Exodus
3	61
3:14–15	61
20:1–5	13

Numbers
4:3	45

Deuteronomy
30	32
30:19–20	32

2 Samuel
22:16	17

1 Kings
3:13	81

2 Kings
6:15–17	75–76

1 Chronicles
29:15	32

2 Chronicles
7:14	90
9:22	81

Scripture Index

Job
11:7	40

Psalms
8	17
19:1–4	9
31:15	32, 67
39:4–6	xxii
66:18–19	91
90:2	108
90:4–6	xxii
90:12	79
102:25–27	96
111:2	8
139:12	1

Proverbs
9:10	84
15:29	91
28:9	90

Ecclesiastes
2:10	81
12	82
12:8	81

Isaiah
6	44
6:1–2	44
6:7	44
40:8	13
42:8–9	13
42:8	13
44:6–8	13
44:6	108
46:9–11	13
51:6	39
53:5	13
55:8–9	71
55:10–11	47–48
55:11	41
64	57
64:4	57
64:6	12, 57, 126
64:7	57
66:24	56

Jeremiah
1:5	68
9:3–5	58
9:6	58
9:14	58
9:23–24	57
9:23	58
9:24	58
17:10	34
29:11–13	92
33:3	90

Ezekiel
1	46
1:1	45
1:4–5	45
1:26–28	45
37–38	xxi

Daniel
2:22	30
9	xxi

Hosea
12	40
12:10	39

Amos
3:7	71

Scripture Index

Micah

5:2	60
6:8	93

NEW TESTAMENT

Matthew

4:10	13
5:16	93
5:17–18	13
5:18	40
5:20	12
5:29–30	125
6	xxi–xxii
6:9–10	91
6:19–21	56
6:33	59
7:13–14	34
7:21–23	13
10:10–39	93
10:32–39	48
12:36	13
13:11	75
16:27	34
26:41	90

Mark

8:36–37	57, 93
8:36	57
11:24	90

Luke

6:35	58
13:3	124
16:9	55–56
21:34–36	93
21:36	90
24:35	52

John

1	48, 54–55, 61
1:1–3	61
1:3	82
1:11	54
1:12	12, 67, 94
1:14	48, 54
3:16–17	12, 125–26
3:18	94
3:36	12, 125
4:14	127
4:24	82
5:18	13
5:24	89
6:9	93
6:35–40	93
6:44	63
6:47	127
6:63	93
8	60–61
8:31–32	77
8:51	60
8:52–53	60
8:54–58	60, 61
8:58	61
8:59	61
10:2–5	84–85
10:9–10	127
10:14	85
10:27	85
10:30	13
14	33
14:6	12, 33, 125
14:8–11	33
14:15	67
15	93
15:15	71
15:16	68
15:19	88
17:1	91
17:4–5	91
17:14–16	88
17:26	91

Acts

2:38–39	12
4:12	12, 126
5:29	13
8:20	13
10:25–26	13
15:18	122
16:31	12, 126
17:11	xix

Scripture Index

Romans

1:16	12
1:18	125
1:20	9, 14
2:6	34
3:20	126
3:20–30	12
3:23	12, 125
4:1–7	12
4:17	86
5	91
5:1	12
5:8	125
5:9–10	13
5:9	127
6:1–2	91
6:23	12, 125
8:1–11	13
8:14–16	94
8:19–23	87
8:30	68
9:11	68
9:16	12
10:9	12
10:11	127
10:13	127
11:6	12
12	88
12:2	88

1 Corinthians

1:27	121
3	13
3:10–15	13
3:13–15	31
3:13	56
3:14–15	56
13	75
13:9–12	75
14:33	41
15:3	13
15:50	87

2 Corinthians

4	71
4:16–18	71
5:1–4	53
5:1	55
5:6	13
5:7	76
5:10–11	13
5:10	34
5:21	13
11:4	106

Galatians

1:3–5	127
2:16–21	12
2:16	126
3:10–12	126
5:4	12
5:13	67
6:8	87

Ephesians

1:4	68
1:11–12	68
1:21–22	13
2:1–5	12
2:8–9	12, 126
2:13–22	12
3:8–12	93
4:17–24	93
5:16	29
6:12	75

Philippians

1:9–10	84
1:21	30
1:22–26	30–31
2:8–10	50
2:9–11	13
3	34
3:4–6	36
3:7–8	31
3:13	34
3:14–15	35
3:20	36
3:21	36
4	90
4:6	90
4:7	90

Scripture Index

Colossians

1	109
1:16–17	108
2	43
2:6–9	84
2:17	43
4:2	90

2 Thessalonians

1:9	13

1 Timothy

2:1	90
2:5	12
6:7	56–57
6:11	58
6:18–19	58

2 Timothy

1:9	12, 68, 126
3:16–17	13
3:16	40

Titus

2:11	12
3:4–7	126
3:4–5	12

Hebrews

4:12	13, 47
4:13	19
7:27	13
8	42
8:4–5	42
8:5	43
9	42
9:1–7	42
9:8–12	42–43
9:24	43
9:27	13
10	xxii, 43
10:1	43
10:10	121
10:12–18	13
11	37, 52–53, 114
11:1–3	37
11:1	37
11:3	108
11:13–16	52
11:39–40	53
12	95
12:2	38

James

1:13–15	67
1:23–25	89
2:10–11	126
4:14	79
5:16	90

1 Peter

2:8	53
3:15	xxiii, 38
3:18	13

2 Peter

1:3–4	87
1:4	95
1:13–14	54
1:20–21	13
1:20	40
2:9	13
3	95
3:3–5	108–9
3:8	xxii, 67
3:9	67, 125
3:10–13	95
3:10	95
3:13	95

1 John

1:9	12
2	80
2:2	68
2:15–17	79–80
2:17	xxi, 31
2:25	127
3:14	89
3:19–20	68
5:11–13	12

Scripture Index

Jude

22–23	58
23	95

Revelation

6:10	52
8:13	52
11	xxi
11:10	52
19–22	95
19:10	13
20:12–14	13
20:13–15	125
21:1–5	94
21:8	13
22	108
22:8–9	13
22:12	34
22:13	62, 108

www.ingramcontent.com/pod-product-compliance
Lightning Source LLC
Chambersburg PA
CBHW051935160426
43198CB00013B/2155